Professor Ann Hartle trains her keen philosophical eye on the deep congruence between Flannery O'Connor's fiction and Blaise Pascal's faith. Pascal's celebrated saying that "The heart has reasons which reason does not know" does not commend an emotional Christianity. Hartle shows that, for both Pascal and O'Connor, the heart is the seat not of soft feeling but of tough thinking and willing and acting. Against Montaigne's detached ratiocination, unmoored from divine revelation, Pascal grounded his theology in the historical reality of the Incarnation. O'Connor joined him in rooting her fiery faith and fiction in "the God of Abraham, Isaac, and Jacob and not of the philosophers and scholars." Like O'Connor, Hartle makes her appeal not only to fellow Catholics but to all who are tempted to discarnate ways of thinking and living. She also refuses to make Christian faith obvious: "The incarnation and the Eucharist," she confesses, "both hide and reveal the historical and embodied presence of Christ in the world." Thus does her ground-breaking book have revolutionary importance for philosophers, theologians, and all lovers of Flannery O'Connor.

Ralph C. Wood is the author of *Flannery O'Connor and the Christ-Haunted South* as well as the forthcoming *Flannery O'Connor and the Church Made Visible*. He is Emeritus Professor of Theology and Literature at Baylor University.

Flannery O'Connor and Blaise Pascal

RECOVERING THE INCARNATION FOR THE MODERN MIND

Flannery O'Connor & Blaise Pascal

RECOVERING THE INCARNATION FOR THE MODERN MIND

Ann Hartle

The Catholic University of America Press
Washington, D.C.

Copyright © 2025

The Catholic University of America Press

All rights reserved

The paper used in this publication meets the minimum
requirements of American National Standards for
Information Science—Permanence of Paper
for Printed Library Materials, ANSI Z39.48-1992.

∞

Cataloging-in-Publication Data is available from the Library of Congress

ISBN: 978-0-8132-3972-9

eISBN: 978-0-8132-3973-6

For my sister, Judith, and my brother-in-law, Raymond

Contents

Acknowledgments ▪ ix

Abbreviations ▪ xi

INTRODUCTION　Pascal in the Protestant South ▪ 1

CHAPTER 1　The Idea and the Mummy:
Hazel Motes's Unhistorical Consciousness ▪ 23

CHAPTER 2　Hulga's Heart Condition:
The Disembodied and Detached Modern Mind ▪ 45

CHAPTER 3　Rayber's Solitary Consciousness ▪ 69

CHAPTER 4　The Head-Doctor and The Misfit's Guilty Conscience ▪ 91

CHAPTER 5　O'Connor's Comic Art of the Possible and
Pascal's True Philosophy ▪ 113

CHAPTER 6　Conversion: From Modern Consciousness to
Christian Consciousness ▪ 137

CHAPTER 7　The Misfit's Prophetic Vision and
Contemporary Culture ▪ 157

Bibliography ▪ 177

Index ▪ 185

Acknowledgments

I wish to thank the staff of the Stuart A. Rose Manuscript, Archives, and Rare Book Library, Emory University for their assistance with my research in the O'Connor-Hester correspondence.

Abbreviations

MMSS   Carl Gustav Jung, *Modern Man in Search of a Soul*, trans. W. S. Dell and Cary F. Baynes (New York: Harcourt, 1933).

US   Carl Gustav Jung, *The Undiscovered Self*, trans. R. F. C. Hull (New York: Signet, 2006).

E   Michel de Montaigne, *The Complete Essays of Montaigne*, trans. Donald Frame (Stanford, CA: Stanford University Press, 1943).

CW   Flannery O'Connor, *The Collected Works*, ed. Sally Fitzgerald (New York: Library of America, 1988).

CS   Flannery O'Connor, *The Complete Stories* (New York: Farrar, Straus and Giroux, 1971).

Conv   Flannery O'Connor, *Conversations with Flannery O'Connor*, ed. Rosemary M. Magee (Jackson and London: University Press of Mississippi, 1987).

HB   Flannery O'Connor, *The Habit of Being*, ed. Sally Fitzgerald (New York: Farrar, Straus and Giroux, 1979).

MM   Flannery O'Connor, *Mystery and Manners*, ed. Sally and Robert Fitzgerald (New York: Farrar, Straus and Giroux, 1961).

PJ   Flannery O'Connor, *A Prayer Journal*, ed. W. A. Sessions (New York: Farrar, Straus and Giroux, 2013).

Pres	Flannery O'Connor, *The Presence of Grace and Other Book Reviews*, Compiled by Leo J. Zuber; ed. Carter W. Martin (Athens: The University of Georgia Press, 1983).
VBA	Flannery O'Connor, *The Violent Bear It Away* (New York: Farrar, Straus and Giroux, 1955).
WB	Flannery O'Connor, *Wise Blood* (New York: Farrar, Straus and Giroux, 2007).
SW	Blaise Pascal, *Great Shorter Works*, trans. Emile Cailliet and John C. Blankenagel (Eugene, OR: Wipf and Stock, 2017.)
P	Blaise Pascal, *Pensées*, trans. A. J. Krailsheimer (London: Penguin Books, 1995).
PL	Blaise Pascal, *The Provincial Letters*, trans. A. J. Krailsheimer (New York: Penguin Books, 1982).

Introduction
Pascal in the Protestant South

What does it mean to be Catholic in the modern world? What is the experience of the believer who wants to understand how faith might make sense of the human condition in a culture which is thoroughly secular and increasingly hostile to Christianity, and to Catholic faith in particular? Flannery O'Connor, in her stories, letters, and essays, illuminates this experience with profound insight and amazing clarity, for this is her own condition, a condition which she confronts directly and in which she finds the possibility of faith.

In a letter to a friend, O'Connor describes herself as a Catholic possessed of the modern consciousness which the psychologist Carl Gustav Jung views as "unhistorical, solitary, and guilty." She experiences this as a burden, but one that is necessary for the "conscious Catholic" to bear. To carry this burden is to experience the contemporary situation "at the ultimate level" (*HB*, 90). O'Connor recognizes this form of consciousness in herself, and her faith must come to terms with it. Because she understands the modern world so clearly, she foresees where the modern distortion of consciousness would lead. Her fiction illuminates our own contemporary situation at the deepest level.

Why Jung, Montaigne, and Pascal

I approach O'Connor's work from a philosophical perspective rather than the perspective of a literary critic. My intention is to understand O'Connor's fiction as her confrontation with the specifically modern form of consciousness displayed in the psychology of Jung. Whether or not Jung's approach to psychiatry has gone out of fashion makes no difference to my argument, for Jung captures the essence of modern consciousness, the form of human consciousness which emerged in early modern philosophy, especially in the *Essays* of the sixteenth-century philosopher Michel de Montaigne. I do not claim that Jung read Montaigne and knowingly adopted his view of self-consciousness but that Jung's psychology is the outcome of the early modern philosophical consciousness which finds its most explicit expression in Montaigne.[1] To understand how O'Connor responds to the modern condition, I turn to one of Montaigne's most trenchant critics: the seventeenth-century philosopher Blaise Pascal. Pascal helps us to experience the meaning of O'Connor's fiction because he confronted that same consciousness in its origins in Montaigne's philosophy. O'Connor recognizes in Pascal a truly Catholic modern philosopher who speaks to the experience of the searching mind of modern man. Pascal thus helps us to experience the meaning of O'Connor's fiction from a philosophical perspective.

My primary audience, then, is the Catholic or the inquirer who seeks to gain a deeper understanding of what it means to live as a Catholic in the modern world. In the process of presenting O'Connor as a guide for such an individual, I hope to shed light on her stories, especially through my discussion of four of her characters who embody the modern ethos as she understands it.

---

1   Barry Ulanov, *Jung and the Outside World* (Asheville, NC: Chiron Press, 1992), 5. Montaigne is the figure who can be closely linked with Jung "for the rigor of his critical examination of himself in his essays and the unquenchable impulse to self-renewal inherent in the criticism."

O'Connor's letters and essays are filled with both favorable and critical references to philosophers, theologians, and poets from every period of history. My intention is not to situate O'Connor within the history of ideas or to trace all of the many philosophical, theological, or literary influences on her work.[2] My focus is on her confrontation with modern consciousness. Therefore, I turn to Jung and Pascal because O'Connor finds in Jung her most comprehensive description of modern consciousness, and she finds in Pascal the philosopher whom she recommends to those struggling to transcend the limits of modern consciousness, specifically the self-consciousness that Pascal encounters in Montaigne. The extent of O'Connor's familiarity with Montaigne's thought is unclear. O'Connor had a copy of the *Selected Essays* of Montaigne in her library.[3] However, she never mentions Montaigne in her letters and essays. Among modern philosophers, Montaigne and Descartes are Pascal's principal adversaries. Although Descartes is indeed representative of the new modern consciousness, he approaches this in terms of the new science and the scientific method. Montaigne's self-examination in his *Essays* is more directly a manifestation of modern consciousness as *self*-consciousness. My appeal to Montaigne is based on Pascal's criticisms of him and on the form of self-consciousness displayed in the *Essays* which ultimately appears in Jungian psychoanalysis.

My method is not that of a literary critic—uncovering the causes of O'Connor's ideas or the sources of her characters and plots—but that of a philosopher, illuminating the meaning of her stories for the searching mind of modern man. I take this approach being aware that O'Connor is primarily an artist, not a theorist. Her stories are not mosaics of philosophical ideas which can be traced back to their genesis in various

---

[2] Some explorations of specific Catholic influences can be found in Mark Bosco, SJ, and Brent Little, eds., *Revelation and Convergence: Flannery O'Connor and the Catholic Intellectual Tradition* (Washington, DC: The Catholic University of America Press, 2017).

[3] Arthur F. Kinney, *Flannery O'Connor's Library: Resources of Being* (Athens: The University of Georgia Press, 1985), 132.

philosophers. She insists that she is "making" something, and the fact that she herself does not fully understand her own stories shows that she is trying to be true to the "mystery" of original sin and redemption. The warrant for my approach is this: the meaning of her stories is greater than any ideas of which she might be conscious.

Although I approach O'Connor's fiction from a philosophical rather than a literary perspective, my goal is not to replace the stories with a philosophical explanation or to abstract a philosophical meaning from the stories. O'Connor insists that the work of art must never be produced by imposing a "system" of thought on the concrete details of reality. Nor should the writer attempt to use any philosophical or theological teaching as the structure upon which to build a story. "You don't begin a story with a system. You can forget about the system. These are things that you believe; they may affect your writing *unconsciously*. I don't think theology should be a scaffolding" (*Conv*, 29). A story should be an *experience* of meaning: "When anybody asks what a story is about, the only proper thing is to tell him to read the story. The meaning of fiction is not abstract meaning but experienced meaning, and *the purpose of making statements about the meaning of a story is only to help you experience the meaning more fully*" (*MM*, 96, emphasis added).

In her correspondence with a young man who is struggling with the possibility of entering the church, O'Connor writes: "I hope you'll find the experience you need to make the leap toward Christianity seem the only one to you. Pascal had a good deal to say about this" (*HB*, 485). It would have to be an *experience*, not an argument, that would make the leap possible. O'Connor's task as a novelist is to create the *experience* of the *possibility* of grace. My goal is to deepen the experience of the meaning of her stories by appealing to Pascal in order to uncover her Catholic assumptions, assumptions which are never stated in the stories but which give them their depth.[4]

---

[4] O'Connor is, however, wary of what she perceives as Pascal's Jansenism. In a letter to a friend, she writes: "I like Pascal but I don't think the Jansenist influence

A Note on Aquinas and Modern Gnosticism

To claim that Pascal can shed light on O'Connor's work is not to deny her indebtedness to St. Thomas Aquinas. Anticipating her appearance on TV in an interview about her novel *Wise Blood*, O'Connor writes: "Everybody who has read *Wise Blood* thinks I'm a hillbilly nihilist, whereas I would like to create the impression over the television that I'm a hillbilly Thomist" (*HB*, 81). Throughout her letters and essays, O'Connor discusses her approach to her work, and especially her understanding of the art of fiction writing, in terms of the teaching of St. Thomas Aquinas. She insists that the fundamental convictions underlying her stories are the dogmas of orthodox Catholic faith and that her mind has been formed by her reading of Thomistic theology.[5]

Marion Montgomery, in his seminal works on O'Connor, accounts for her description of herself as a "hillbilly Thomist" in light of her confrontation with the heresy of Gnosticism which has posed a threat to Christianity from its earliest centuries. The term "Gnosticism" comes from the Greek word for "knowledge." But the kind of knowledge sought by the adherents of Gnosticism is a knowledge that claims to surpass the condition of faith. The Gnostics claimed to offer a superior understanding of Scripture available only to the most intelligent, superior souls capable of rising above the traditional crude beliefs and practices of the church. Manicheanism, a sect which St. Augustine confronted in

---

is healthy in the Church" (*HB*, 304). She goes on to explain that the Irish (her own people) are very much infected with Jansenism which "doesn't seem to breed so much a love of God as a love of asceticism" (*HB*, 304). In spite of her awareness of this danger, she confesses that her upbringing "has smacked a little of Jansenism." Yet her convictions, she insists, have not been formed by Jansenism (*HB*, 117).

5   Fr. Damian Ference, in his *Understanding the Hillbilly Thomist: The Philosophical Foundations of Flannery O'Connor's Narrative Art* (Elk Grove Village, IL: Word on Fire, 2023), offers a systematic overview of O'Connor's stories and her practice of the art of writing in terms of Aquinas's metaphysics, epistemology, and ethics.

the fourth century, is a form of Gnosticism. Manicheanism is the belief that matter is evil, holding the human being back from the perfection of his mind. Throughout the ages, Gnosticism has taken various forms, all of them centering on the separation of spirit and matter for the sake of this superior knowledge. Initiates into this higher knowledge were held to be "spiritual" souls who alone possessed the true understanding of Scripture, of the meaning of the incarnation, and of the meaning of human being.

Montgomery identifies a specifically modern form of Gnosticism in which Scripture and the incarnation are used to make the self absolute. Modern Gnosticism, he says, attempts to accomplish the separation of spirit and matter through the power of the human mind itself. The modern Gnostic believes that by his intellect "he can perform his own resurrection, an intellectual act whereby he rises above existence."[6] And through this separation of consciousness from existence, the self becomes absolute.[7]

My argument is that modern consciousness rests on the "spiritualization" of the incarnation. Both Montaigne and Jung abstract a purely human meaning from the historical embodied reality of the incarnation and place that meaning in the service of modern man's attempt at self-creation and self-redemption. Montaigne presents his discovery of self-consciousness as a radical break with the Christian tradition in which one "dies" to his old self and is resurrected by his own power as a new kind of man. Jung says that the "deepest sense" of "unhistorical" is to break with the tradition in order to re-create oneself. The unhistorical consciousness is necessarily solitary and guilty because the break with tradition is experienced as an ethical break: the new modern man separates himself from the

---

6   Marion Montgomery, *The Trouble with You Innerleckchuls* (Front Royal, VA: Christendom College Press, 1988), 4.

7   Montgomery, *Innerleckchuls*, 17.

human community for he does not judge himself by the common moral standard of the tradition but by his own higher and private standard of self-creation. Jung denies the historical reality of the incarnation, turning it into a mere idea or symbol which is essential for psychological health. Both Pascal and O'Connor see their task as the recovery of the historical embodied reality of the incarnation for the modern mind from the distortions of this spiritualization.

The modern Gnostic spiritualization of the incarnation is the basis for the modern unhistorical consciousness which O'Connor finds in Jung and which Pascal confronts in Montaigne. In *The Incarnational Art of Flannery O'Connor*, Christina Bieber Lake provides the description of this modern Gnosticism which is central to my argument. Gnosticism "spiritualizes the Incarnation so that its meaning for humanity trumps the event as part of actual human history."[8]

Pascal, then, is especially helpful for understanding O'Connor's response to modern Gnosticism. With respect to matters of faith, both Aquinas and Pascal believe what the church teaches. Both express the same eternal truth which cannot be captured fully in any system of thought. Yet, in viewing O'Connor's work through a Pascalian lens, certain aspects of her penetration of the mystery of human existence come to the fore and are made explicit, aspects which might remain only implicit when her work is viewed through a Thomistic lens.

The Relevance of Pascal

O'Connor was very much aware of the meaning of modern philosophy and its implications for faith and culture. In his biography of O'Connor, Brad Gooch records the judgment of Helen Matthews Lewis who knew

---

8   Christina Bieber Lake, *The Incarnational Art of Flannery O'Connor* (Macon, GA: Mercer University Press, 2005), 5.

O'Connor well while she was a student at Georgia State College for Women. The textbook for their course on modern philosophy, John Herman Randall's *The Making of the Modern Mind*, focused on the transition from medieval to modern philosophy. According to Lewis, O'Connor believed that "it was philosophical *modernism* that had blinded the Western mind."[9]

Pascal is perhaps the first philosopher who criticizes the fundamental direction of modern philosophy. He is, therefore, the philosopher who can help us to experience the meaning of her stories insofar as they are addressed to a specifically modern audience. Pascal paints for us the intellectual and cultural background of modernity within which O'Connor's stories are set. He stands behind her vision of the human condition and the meaning of human existence in the modern world. Pascal's unfinished apology for the Christian religion is his defense of the possibility of faith in the modern world.

I understand Pascal's Christian consciousness in light of his struggle with Montaigne, who has been described as "the great adversary against whom Pascal set himself."[10] In particular, "Pascal confronts Montaigne as an adversary of the way of thinking and way of life he finds embedded in the *Essays*, and which are contrary to the true Christian religion."[11] The structure of the Christian consciousness of Pascal's *Pensées* takes shape in his encounter with Montaigne. As Benjamin and Jenna Storey explain: "No one has given more powerful voice to ... suspicions of Montaignean moral modernism than Blaise Pascal. At modernity's outset, Pascal

---

9   Brad Gooch, *Flannery: A Life of Flannery O'Connor* (New York: Little, Brown and Company, 2009), 114.

10   T. S. Eliot, "The *Pensées* of Pascal," in *Selected Essays* (New York: Harcourt Brace, 1932), 362.

11   Henry Phillips, "Pascal's Reading and the Inheritance of Montaigne and Descartes," in *Cambridge Companion to Pascal*, ed. Nicholas Hammond (Cambridge: Cambridge University Press, 2003), 24.

examines its meaning in all of its dimensions, with a penetration few have been able to match."[12]

In his essay on the *Pensées*, T. S. Eliot says of Pascal: "I know of no religious writer more pertinent to our time.... I can think of no Christian writer ... more to be commended than Pascal to those who doubt, but who have the mind to conceive, and the sensibility to feel, the disorder, the futility, the meaninglessness, the mystery of life and suffering, and who can only find peace through a satisfaction of the whole being."[13]

Romano Guardini, in *The End of the Modern World*, concludes that Pascal "is related to the modern world in a manner distinctly his own, in a manner proper to one who was both a psychologist and a philosopher of the meaning of Christian existence. He belongs to that company of men who saw the whole situation of the new world which was coming to be," assumed a critical attitude toward that world, and formulated a philosophy and an ethics whose significance is only now being fully revealed.[14] Pascal meets the condition of the man who can help us to understand ourselves in our own time, the condition "that he be situated in real history; that his time live in him, and that he feel himself impelled to justify his believing existence in it."[15]

Pascal's time lived in him. He was very much a participant in the scientific revolution of the seventeenth century, corresponding and meeting with some of the most prominent scientists and mathematicians of his day. At sixteen, he wrote an essay on conic sections, and later he worked out

---

12   Benjamin Storey and Jenna Silber Storey, *Why We Are Restless: On the Modern Quest for Contentment* (Princeton, NJ and Oxford: Princeton University Press, 2021), 52.
13   Eliot, "The *Pensées* of Pascal," 368.
14   Romano Guardini, *The End of the Modern World*, trans. Joseph Theman and Herbert Burke (Wilmington, DE: ISI Books, 1998), xxiv.
15   Romano Guardini, *Pascal for Our Time*, trans. Brian Thompson (New York: Herder and Herder, 1966), 9.

the foundation for the infinitesimal calculus, the integral calculus, and the calculus of probabilities, all in advance of the accomplishments of Newton and Leibniz. He built the first mechanical calculating machine. And his study of atmospheric pressure resulted in what is known as Pascal's Law. Pascal's works on physics are "still admired for their rigour and held up as models of empirical investigation."[16]

In addition to his writings on mathematics and science, Pascal wrote a polemical work, *The Provincial Letters* (in which he defends the Jansenists of Port Royal against their Jesuit opponents) and several shorter works on philosophical and religious topics. His most important philosophical work is his unfinished apology for the Christian religion, which came to be called the *Pensées*, a collection of fragments for this apology, discovered after his death.

In spite of his strong attraction to and his great success in the practice of natural science, Pascal concluded that these "abstract sciences" were not appropriate for the study of man. In his insistence on the limitations of modern science and his conviction that only the incarnation can teach us our true nature and our true condition, Pascal is at one with O'Connor in confronting the distortions of modern consciousness. Both are very much aware that their task is one of recovery from the effects of modern consciousness and that the recovery cannot be simply a return to or repetition of pre-modern forms of thought. For both Pascal and O'Connor, the recovery of the reality of the incarnation for the modern mind must take a new form.

O'Connor gives us a glimpse of what this new form might be in her review of Barry Ulanov's *Seeds of Hope in the Modern World*. She praises the author for offering "an antidote to a tendency of Catholics to despise the modern world on principle and to condemn out of hand anything

---

16 Daniel C. Fouke, "Pascal's Physics," in *Cambridge Companion to Pascal*, ed. Nicholas Hammond (Cambridge: Cambridge University Press, 2003), 75.

that does not have obvious roots in the Middle Ages." The book, she says, achieves its purpose, "which is to suggest the potential power of the modern world to lead a man closer to God." In her presentation of Ulanov's description of the best modern meditative minds, she may well be giving us insight into her understanding of her own work: "The remarkable meditative minds of our time ... have looked through the familiar to the unfamiliar, have looked with such intensity and ingenuity and patience at the commonplace that they have discovered once again ... how very uncommon it is" (*Pres*, 158–59).

O'Connor describes her work as "a descent through the darkness of the familiar" (*MM*, 50). For O'Connor and Pascal, "the familiar" is the moral world, the world of human action and inter-action, as it is encountered in modern life. Both O'Connor and Pascal descend through the familiar moral world to the mysteries of original sin and redemption.

A Catholic Vision of the Protestant South

When O'Connor says that the fiction writer must begin with the familiar, she specifies that it is the moral world of the Protestant South which is most familiar to her. This is her gateway to reality in the modern world. For the prophets and freaks of her stories, the drama of salvation is played out on the landscape of the Protestant South of her day. When O'Connor looks through the familiar, she sees beyond her region to her "true country," to the "eternal and absolute" (*MM*, 27).

As a Catholic born and raised in the Protestant South, she is "both native and alien" (*MM*, 197). While she is thoroughly familiar with and observes the mores and manners of the culture, as a Catholic, she has a certain distance from it. This distance was increased by her time in graduate school in Iowa and living near New York City, before illness forced her home. Finally, as a novelist, she "stands apart from experience" (*HB*, 184) in order to "contemplate experience, not [be] merged in it" (*MM*,

84). As she explains in an interview, "I think that to overcome regionalism, you must have a great deal of self-knowledge. I think to know yourself is to know your region, and that it's also to know the world, and in a sense, paradoxically, it's also to be in exile from that world. So that you have a great deal of detachment" (*Conv*, 8). This means that "the Georgia writer's true country is not Georgia, but Georgia is an entrance to it for him. One uses the region in order to suggest what transcends it." Her own gaze extends to "that realm of mystery which is the concern of prophets" (*Conv*, 110).

In *Why Flannery O'Connor Stayed Home*, Marion Montgomery claims that "her genius is such that, recognizing that the South has long belonged to that larger view of human existence, she could defend that view in the place where she was at home. The critic who laments the intrusion upon her of disseminated lupus because it required her to live at Andalusia, just outside Milledgeville, Georgia, in the provincial South, has not yet begun to understand either the South or Flannery O'Connor."[17]

The South is O'Connor's gateway to reality primarily because a remnant of the pre-modern historical consciousness is still pervasive there. On account of the Civil War, there persisted a historical consciousness of defeat and fallenness.[18] More fundamentally, the history of salvation is still openly acknowledged there. O'Connor says, "it takes a story to make a story.... In the Protestant South, the Scriptures fill this role" (*MM*, 202).

---

17 Marion Montgomery, *Why Flannery O'Connor Stayed Home*, vol. 1, *The Prophetic Poet and the Spirit of the Age* (La Salle, IL: Sherwood Sugden and Company, 1981), 34.

18 O'Connor understood that this sense of "fallenness" is tied not simply to defeat in the Civil War but to the evil of the practice of slavery. A thorough-going examination of O'Connor's writings with respect to the issue of race is beyond the scope of this book. Suffice it to say here that, in her reflections on race, her historical consciousness as a Southerner is framed in terms of the history of salvation and our dependence upon each other in the economy of salvation.

The Bible creates the common culture of her region so that the story that is behind all of her stories—the story of original sin and redemption—gives them the depth of meaning that is possible only where they can be read against the background of a common understanding of human life. In particular, she can use the Old Testament as her background because the idea of the prophet was still alive and familiar in the public culture (*Conv*, 59). "The Bible is what we share with all Christians, and the Old Testament we share with all Jews" (*Conv*, 87). Indeed, "the Hebrew genius for making the absolute concrete has conditioned the Southerner's way of looking at things" (*MM*, 202).

O'Connor knows full well that her backwoods prophets will be looked down upon by the readers that she always kept in mind—the liberal elites of the more sophisticated regions of the country. Referring to a review of *The Violent Bear It Away*, she notes that the reviewer calls Tarwater the latest addition to her "band of poor God-driven Southern whites." O'Connor writes: "I am getting the connection between the God-driven and the underprivileged—God-drivenness being a form of Southern degeneracy" (*HB*, 371). But this is the farthest thing from her own view of her characters: "The Bible gives meaning and dignity to the lives of the poor people of the South, and the writer, particularly the Christian writer, has something in common with them" (*Conv*, 83).

Ralph C. Wood, in his *Flannery O'Connor and the Christ-Haunted South*, explains O'Connor's affinity with fundamentalist Protestants in terms of her reaction to the American cultural milieu of the 1950s. Liberal Protestantism watered down the doctrinal clarity of Christian belief in "modifications of the gospel that would make it fit modern needs."[19] Liberal Protestants sought to foster a kind of civil religion by ignoring theological differences for the sake of social peace and justice. Thus, Wood

---

19   Ralph C. Wood, *Flannery O'Connor and the Christ-Haunted South* (Grand Rapids, MI: William B. Eerdmans Publishing Company, 2004), 11.

claims, particular historic faiths melted into a thin religious gruel.[20] "This code of civility denies all radical and exclusive claims to religious finality, turning authoritative revelation and tradition into pluralist and individualist 'choices'."[21]

O'Connor's portrayal of fundamentalists, then, is not (as it may first appear) a satirical attack but rather a subtle defense of the fundamentalists' unapologetic Christianity and deep veneration of Scripture. In this way, there is a strong bond between orthodox Catholics and backwoods fundamentalists. Wood quotes O'Connor's judgment that "it is an embarrassment to our fundamentalist neighbors to realize that they are doctrinally nearer their traditional enemy, the Church of Rome, than they are to modern Protestantism. The day may come when Catholics will be the ones who maintain the spiritual traditions of the South" (*Pres*, 77).

With respect to her specifically Catholic response to the spiritualization of the incarnation, it should go without saying that O'Connor's Catholic view of human life does not imply that Protestants are not really Christians, for Protestants belong to the invisible church. Nor does it imply that holiness and charity are found only in members of the visible church: charity and holiness can be found everywhere when grace is at work. Her characters are usually Protestant, and this works well because the relationship between the individual and the person of Jesus Christ is of the greatest importance, and that is what she is after in her stories.

O'Connor writes about Protestants, rather than Catholics, not only because she lives in the Protestant South but also because "conversion within the Church ... is a more difficult subject than conversion without" (*HB*, 113). The Protestant's relationship to God is not mediated through the sacraments of the church: it is a direct relationship to God which can show itself more dramatically in the visible actions of the individual. Indeed,

---

20 Wood, 17–18.
21 Wood, 22.

O'Connor says that she can write about Protestant believers better than about Catholic believers "because they express their belief in diverse kinds of dramatic action which is obvious enough for me to catch" (*HB*, 517). Catholic writers who don't use Catholic settings or characters "are trying to make it plain that personal loyalty to the person of Christ is imperative, is the structure of man's nature, his necessary direction, etc. The Church, as institution, doesn't come into it one way or another" (*HB*, 290). As she says of Old Tarwater: "He lacks the visible Church, but Christ is the center of his life" (*Conv*, 83). Protestants reject the authoritative status of the tradition as it is maintained by the Catholic church for they accept only the authority of Scripture. Nevertheless, the core of the tradition is preserved for them in their steadfast belief in the divinity and the historical reality of Christ. So, although she writes about Protestants because the personal relationship with Christ is central, the tradition stands behind her stories because only the presence of the tradition, in whatever way it is transmitted, can ground the personal relationship in reality and truth: tradition transmits the reality of the Christian mystery.[22]

On the other hand, the modern tendency to separate spirit and matter is also present in "the Protestant temper" which believes in "approaching the spiritual directly instead of through matter" (*HB*, 304). In this way, the Protestant view rejects the Catholic tradition of seeing the high in the low, the spiritual in the material, and grace in nature. The "Protestant temper" is such that the sacraments and the principle of mutual interdependence (essential to the Catholic understanding of Christian community) are not regarded as central to the Christian

---

[22] M. K. Shaddix, *The Church without the Church: Desert Orthodoxy in Flannery O'Connor's "Dear Old Dirty Southland"* (Macon, GA: Mercer University Press, 2015), xii. "O'Connor believed that writing catholically was … [about] realizing the 'invisible Church' in the fullness of its reality." Shaddix discusses the connections of O'Connor's stories with Orthodox sacramentalism in contrast with "the intellectualization of the Incarnation" (xiv).

life. O'Connor says that this rejection of our mutual interdependence is "highly Protestant" (*HB*, 102). Her characters, however, in spite of their human imperfections, are means of grace to each other and thus manifest the Catholic teaching of the communion of saints. O'Connor's vision of human life is focused on the central mystery of the incarnation and our participation in the divine life. For the Catholic, this participation is primarily through the sacramental life of the church, the center of which is the Eucharist (*HB*, 346). O'Connor's vision, then, is "the Catholic sacramental view of life" (*MM*, 152).

Referring to Hazel Motes, the reluctant prophet in *Wise Blood*, she writes: "Haze is saved by virtue of having wise blood; it's too wise for him ultimately to deny Christ. Wise blood has to be these people's means of grace—they have no sacraments" (*HB*, 350). Grace, for Hazel Motes, comes through his blood, through his embodiment. The sacramental view of life, then, is not limited to the sacraments as such. Rather it extends to the very embodiment of the human being. For O'Connor the mystery of human existence, the mystery of personality, the mystery of freedom are experienced in the union of spirit and matter.

When O'Connor says that her view of life is the Catholic sacramental view, her point, I believe, is that only the Catholic sacramental view of human life can give us the most complete context for the meaning of the mystery of human existence. It expresses the way in which spirit and matter, nature and grace, are inseparable, and it places the drama of human action within the most comprehensive framework of Christ's plan of salvation. In *Wise Blood*, Hazel Motes's obsession with the redeeming blood of Christ leads him back to the historical embodied reality of the incarnation. In *The Violent Bear It Away*, the Tarwaters cannot escape their all-consuming hunger for the bread of life. In this way, the Catholic sacramental view of life permeates her stories despite the absence of visible sacraments.

The Structure of This Book

This book is structured in two parts—first, modern consciousness and second, the recovery of the incarnation—although both themes weave throughout the book. In chapters 1 through 4, I set out the characteristics of the modern individual whose consciousness is unhistorical, solitary, and guilty, as these appear in four of O'Connor's characters. I locate the source of these characteristics in Montaigne and Jung, and I show how Pascal and O'Connor respond to these features of modern consciousness. In chapters 5, 6, and 7, I discuss the recovery of the reality of the incarnation in O'Connor's art, in the meaning of Christian conversion, and in the specifically Catholic response to contemporary culture.

Chapter 1: The Idea and the Mummy: Hazel Motes's Unhistorical Consciousness

In *Wise Blood*, the unhistorical consciousness of Hazel Motes reveals itself in the fact that Haze rejects the tradition: he wants to found a new church, and so he needs a "new jesus." This new jesus is presented to Haze in the form of Enoch Emery's mummy and Onnie Jay Holy's idea. The "idea" is the product of the spiritualization of the incarnation; the mummy is man without God. Haze's integrity consists in his refusal to accept either the mummy or the idea as the jesus he is looking for. In the end, he finds the true meaning of the incarnation in the historical embodied Christ.

For O'Connor, the incarnation is the unique historical intervention on which everything depends. She takes her own bearings from Catholic doctrine because, far from being a hindrance to seeing the world as it is, the tradition preserves mystery for the human mind. In Pascal's philosophy, the primacy of the historical reality of the incarnation for understanding the world and human existence can be seen in his recovery of the meaning of the incarnation from Montaigne's reduction of Catholic tradition to mere custom.

Chapter 2: Hulga's Heart Condition:
The Disembodied and Detached Modern Mind

In "Good Country People," the character of Hulga gives us a clear picture of the detached and disembodied modern mind which is the achievement of Montaigne's self-consciousness. Hulga has a PhD in philosophy: her education has turned her into an atheist and a nihilist. In the scene in which Hulga sets out to seduce a Bible salesman, O'Connor shows us concretely the meaning of "self-consciousness" and the detached attitude of the modern mind in the midst of what should be an erotic experience.

In the act of achieving self-consciousness, the human being becomes the "objective observer-passive subject" of Montaigne's philosophy and of Jung's psychology. What is lost in the turn to modern self-consciousness is what Pascal calls "the heart" which appears in O'Connor's stories as the "blood" or "felt-knowledge." The heart is the embodied form of knowing which opens the human being to something greater than himself. For Pascal, "faith is God perceived by the heart" not by the mind. The distortions of modern self-consciousness can be overcome only in the recovery of the heart.

Chapter 3: Rayber's Solitary Consciousness

The character of Rayber in *The Violent Bear It Away* gives us a more complete picture of modern self-consciousness. Jung says that the consciousness of the modern individual is solitary at all times. Rayber is a psychologist who believes himself to be self-sufficient and self-contained. The basis for the belief that the self-conscious individual is self-sufficient is found in Montaigne who tells us that his principal aim is to be contained within himself and not dependent on anyone else for his fulfillment. In fact, however, Rayber is deeply divided within himself on account of his love for his son, a love which he must regard as "irrational." On the one hand, O'Connor displays in the character of Rayber the profound distortions of the personality of the modern man. On the other hand, the novel reveals the integrity of mind and heart in young Tarwater as he struggles with and finally accepts the offering of divine grace.

Chapter 4: The Head-Doctor and The Misfit's Guilty Conscience

In his encounter with the Grandmother in "A Good Man is Hard to Find," The Misfit reveals a more profound understanding of his guilt than does the psychiatrist at the penitentiary who had diagnosed The Misfit's guilt in the terms of Freudian psychology. The Misfit sees his guilt in the light of original sin and he realizes that the incarnation has made it necessary for him to choose between good and evil. Pascal insists on the inadequacy of modern science to account for the mystery of human existence, for modern science gives us a world in which the human being is not at home, does not "fit," on account of original sin. Like Pascal, O'Connor sees the freak as the figure of our essential "displacement." She brings out the mystery of original sin, of human freedom, and of the possibility of redemption against the background of the deterministic explanations of modern psychology.

Chapter 5: O'Connor's Comic Art of the Possible and Pascal's True Philosophy

Pascal and O'Connor identify the same primary audience: the modern man who is searching for God within a culture that is indifferent to the mystery of human existence. O'Connor's fiction is comic in Dante's sense of comedy, for the possibility of grace is always offered. However, she recognizes that Dante's approach to the most fundamental questions of human life cannot be effective in the modern world because her modern audience is so different from Dante's fourteenth-century readers. Given her indifferent and skeptical audience, which does not believe in eternity or any "other world," O'Connor must accomplish everything in this world, in her own time and place. To restore spiritual contingency is to take the way of the possible, bringing out the possible in the actual. Her way is not to ascend to paradise but to descend into the most concrete details of the here and now in this world.

O'Connor must bring out the possibility of grace against the background of the pervasive psychological attitude toward human conduct. The mystery of human freedom appears in the choice that the character must make when grace is offered. Pascal's "wager" gives us insight into what this choice entails and what it means for the modern individual.

Chapter 6: Conversion: From Modern Consciousness to Christian Consciousness

Christian conversion is the shifting of the center of one's existence from the self to Christ. For the modern individual, this movement must begin in a radical rejection of the absoluteness of the self, a rejection so complete that Pascal describes it as self-hatred and self-annihilation and O'Connor describes it as self-abandonment. Paradoxically, the human being becomes his true self when Christ becomes the center of his consciousness. In this transformation, the psychological difficulties of life are not necessarily eliminated, but they are given their place within the order of the heart, the order of holiness. For both Pascal and O'Connor, conversion begins in self-annihilation and ends in Christian charity, that is, in the love for Christ and for the image of Christ in others.

Chapter 7: The Misfit's Prophetic Vision and Contemporary Culture

What does O'Connor show us about what it means to be Catholic in the modern world? The progress of modernity has brought us to the point where the public presence and authoritative voice of Christianity with respect to morals have been suppressed. In particular, belief in and defense of the worth of the individual human being have been cut off from belief in the incarnation. It is The Misfit who sees this clearly: the choice he must make is the choice between following Christ and murdering an entire family. The presence of Catholic faith in the modern world is manifested in the affirmation of the essential connection between faith in the historical reality of the incarnation and the moral imperative of the worth of even the lowliest and most powerless human being.

1. The Idea and the Mummy: Hazel Motes's Unhistorical Consciousness

Flannery O'Connor confronts modern consciousness in the psychology of Carl Gustav Jung because she sees the pervasiveness of the psychological attitude in modern life: it is the "climate" in which we live and breathe. Indeed, she recognizes this modern consciousness within herself, explaining what this means in a letter to her friend: "When I call myself a Catholic with a modern consciousness, I don't mean what might be implied in the phrase 'modern Catholic,' which doesn't make sense. If you're a Catholic you believe what the Church teaches and the climate makes no difference. What I mean is that I am conscious in a general way of the world's present historical position, which according to Jung is unhistorical" (*HB*, 103).[1]

---

1 For a thorough discussion of O'Connor and the so-called "Modernist" heresy, see George Piggford, "Flannery O'Connor, Friedrich von Hugel, and 'This Modernist Business'," in *A Political Companion to Flannery O'Connor*, ed.

In another letter to this friend, she writes: "I am a Catholic peculiarly possessed of the modern consciousness, that thing Jung describes as unhistorical, solitary, and guilty. To possess this *within* the Church is to bear a burden, the necessary burden for the conscious Catholic. It's to feel the contemporary situation at the ultimate level" (*HB*, 90). In addressing Jung, then, O'Connor comes to grips with modern consciousness at what she holds to be "the ultimate level," the level of the clearest and most complete expression of the meaning of modern consciousness.

Jung says that the "deepest sense" of 'unhistorical' is to break with the tradition in order to re-create oneself (*MMSS*, 197). The tradition, then, is historical consciousness in the deepest sense. The unhistorical consciousness is necessarily solitary and guilty because the break with tradition is experienced as an ethical break: the new modern man separates himself from the human community for he does not judge by the common moral standard of the tradition but by his own higher and private standard of self-creation.

The source of Jung's modern unhistorical consciousness is the "spiritualization" of the incarnation, a radical break with the tradition, for it is the abstraction of a purely human meaning from the historical embodied reality of the incarnation which is the core of the tradition. Jung denies the historical reality of the incarnation, turning it into a mere idea or symbol which is essential for psychological health.

The spiritualization of the incarnation in the service of human perfection is a form of Gnosticism, a heresy which Christianity has had to confront since its earliest centuries. In his introduction to *The Scandal of the Incarnation: Irenaeus "Against the Heretics,"* Hans Urs von Balthasar identifies "the fundamental dogma of Gnosticism—the belief that the lower, material

---

Henry T. Edmondson (Lexington: University of Kentucky, 2017), 101–24. Piggford explains how O'Connor admires von Hugel but does not adopt any of his possibly heretical opinions.

sphere, the 'flesh', the world of the 'psychic', was contemptible, something to be vanquished, while the higher, spiritual world was all that was excellent, the only thing worth cultivating."[2] In the early centuries of Christianity, Gnosticism's "spiritualizing" flight from matter and the flesh is exposed by Irenaeus as "an essentially anti-Christian religious experiment which destroys the psychosomatic unity of man."[3] Gnosticism, then, brings about a division within the individual human being between what is lowest and what is highest, between spirit and matter, mind and body. There is, then, an essential link between the unhistorical consciousness and Gnosticism: "A faith that discards history in this manner really turns into 'Gnosticism.' It leaves flesh, incarnation—just what true history is—behind."[4]

Further, Gnosticism produces a fundamental distinction between two kinds of human beings: "The Gnostics taught that human beings fall into two groups, the higher 'spiritual' and the lower 'carnal' or 'animal', of which only the former can partake of true and complete redemption. Consistently with this, they also taught that the material and bodily elements in the spiritual man are just an inessential shell, which is incapable of entering into the pure spirit's final state of perfection."[5]

The real incarnation, the real suffering of Christ on the cross, and the real resurrection of the flesh, upon which redemption depends, are all a scandal for Gnosticism, for the Gnostic mind can be satisfied only with a God who is spirit. However, for the Christian who seeks the divine, "the flesh is the hinge, the decisive criterion of salvation."[6] Von Balthasar

---

2   Hans Urs von Balthasar, introduction to *The Scandal of the Incarnation: Irenaeus "Against the Heretics"*, by Irenaeus, ed. Hans Urs von Balthasar, trans. John Saward (San Francisco: Ignatius Press, 1981), 1.
3   Von Balthasar, 8.
4   Joseph Ratzinger, *Jesus of Nazareth: From the Baptism in the Jordan to the Transfiguration*, trans. Adrian J. Walker (San Francisco: Ignatius Press, 2007), 228.
5   Von Balthasar, *The Scandal of the Incarnation*, 94.
6   Von Balthasar, introduction, 3–4.

describes the "realism" of the confrontation with Gnosticism: "In contrast to the Gnostics' empty spiritualism and proud contempt for the body, [the Christian realist] stubbornly refuses to let man cut himself off from the life of this world and escape into a pseudo-heavenly half-existence.... If there is to be real redemption, this earth and no other, this body and no other, must have the capacity to take God's grace into itself."[7]

Von Balthasar sees the confrontation between Gnosticism and the incarnation as a confrontation which has persisted and is constantly assuming new forms.[8] The form which Gnosticism takes in the modern world can be clearly seen in O'Connor's first novel, *Wise Blood*, where she confronts directly the spiritualization of the incarnation and the denial of the historical reality of the incarnation.

Hazel Motes is a modern man. His character is "a remarkable portrait of the Western intellectual."[9] O'Connor says that "Haze, even though a primitive, is full of the poison of the modern world" (*HB*, 403). His obsession with Jesus manifests itself as his search for a "new jesus." As Christina Bieber Lake explains, Haze is a modern man because he wants to break with the tradition by founding a new church.[10] Haze proclaims: "I'm going to preach a new church—the church of truth without Jesus Christ Crucified. It won't cost you nothing to join my church" (*WB*, 51). It is specifically the crucifixion of Christ that must be denied in the founding of this new church. "It won't cost you nothing" because there is no crucifixion, no price that Christ paid. You owe him nothing. Of course, Haze resists the real Jesus who demands everything of him, but he really already knows that it costs everything to follow the real Jesus. Haze already knows because his wise blood is the presence of the tradition within him. His blood is *wise* because it is the

---

7 Von Balthasar, 13.
8 Von Balthasar, 4.
9 Marion Montgomery, "Flannery O'Connor: Prophetic Prophet," *The Flannery O'Connor Bulletin* 3 (Autumn 1974): 84.
10 Lake, *Incarnational Art*, 69–70.

"felt-knowledge" (*WB*, 491) of the truth of the tradition, inherited from his grandfather. From the outset, then, we see in Haze the fundamental conflict between tradition and the modern mind. Haze is a reluctant prophet.

The new church needs a new jesus: "I believe in a new kind of jesus," he said, "one that can't waste his blood redeeming people with it, because he's all man and ain't got any God in him. My church is the Church Without Christ" (*WB*, 119). Denying Christ means denying the divinity of Christ: the new jesus is "all man." In Haze's new church, there is no redemption because there is no need for redemption: there is "no Fall because there was nothing to fall from and no Redemption because there was no Fall and no Judgment because there wasn't the first two. Nothing matters but that Jesus was a liar." Haze's new church is "the church that the blood of Jesus don't foul with redemption" (*WB*, 101).

The "church of truth," then, must reject the Jesus who claimed to be God, but it does need a new kind of jesus who can be easily recognized. Haze preaches: "What you need is something to take the place of Jesus, something that would speak plain. The Church Without Christ don't have a Jesus but it needs one! It needs a new jesus! It needs one that's all man, without blood to waste, and it needs one that don't look like any other man so you'll look at him" (*WB*, 140–41). The new jesus must be all man, yet he must not look like any other man. He must, then, be a new man and he must "speak plain," leaving no uncertainty about his fully human status, eliminating all mystery about a divine being who would shed his blood for men, thus denying the claim that Jesus has on us.

The true meaning of the new jesus is revealed to Haze in two ways, in his encounters with Enoch Emery and with Onnie Jay Holy. Enoch operates entirely on the level of instinct; Onnie Jay operates on the level of the mind. Enoch shows Haze the new jesus as a shriveled bloodless mummy; Onnie Jay shows him the new jesus as "a good idea."

It is Enoch who first introduces the notion of "wise blood" in the novel. Enoch "knew by his blood. He had wise blood like his daddy" (*WB*,

75). His inherited, instinctual wisdom was something he could not really articulate. In his wise blood, O'Connor is displaying the unreflective knowledge, the "felt-knowledge" (*WB*, 491), embodied in instinct and manifested in Enoch's openness to mystery.

Enoch works as a guard at the city park and often visits the museum in the center of the park where he discovers a fascinating mummy. He just knows that the mummy in the case in the museum must be the "new jesus" that Haze is seeking, and he is driven to steal the mummy by a desire he does not understand. Inside him was "a terrible knowledge without any words in it." The meaning of the mummy is "a mystery" to him (*WB*, 77). His compulsion to steal it filled him with a sense of doom. This was a mystery beyond his understanding, and he knew that what was going to be expected of him was something awful and that he needed to take the mummy to Haze.

But Haze, in anger and disgust, throws the mummy against the wall, splitting it open so that the trash inside sprays out in a cloud of dust. Haze sees the meaning of his new jesus who is "all man" and he cannot accept this lifeless, bloodless, shrunken man as the jesus he needs. In a letter to Betty Hester, O'Connor explains: "That Haze rejects that mummy suggests everything. What he has been looking for with body and soul throughout the book is suddenly presented to him and he sees it has to be rejected, he sees it ain't really what he's looking for" (*HB*, 404).

On one occasion when Haze is preaching his new church from the platform of the roof of his car, he draws a small crowd of people among whom is Onnie Jay Holy. Onnie Jay sees immediately the potential in this new church to make some money, so he seizes the opportunity and begins to talk to the crowd on Haze's behalf. The new jesus for this new church is all sweetness and light, the perfect jesus for original, uncorrupted human nature. "Every person that comes onto this earth is born sweet and full of love … its nature is sweetness—until something happens" (*WB*, 150). Onnie Jay himself is just overflowing with love for everyone, but he needs "a new jesus to help me bring my sweet nature into the open" (*WB*, 151). Onnie Jay's idea of jesus is man without original sin.

It's really easy to believe in this new jesus and join his new church for there is no mystery to trouble your mind: "You don't have to believe nothing you don't understand and approve of" (*WB*, 152). Onnie Jay assures the crowd: "This church is up-to-date!" (*WB*, 153) For his second appearance at Haze's street preaching, Onnie Jay hires his own preacher to compete with Haze by preaching this up-to-date church: "The unredeemed are redeeming theirselves and the new jesus is at hand! Watch for this miracle!" (*WB*, 167)

Haze is furious at Onnie Jay and the new preacher because they are not preaching the truth. But Onnie Jay tries to reason with him: "You got good idears, … I never heard a idear before that had more in it than that one. All it would need is a little promotion.… I kind of have had that idear about a new jesus myself" (*WB*, 157). At this point, Haze is compelled to deny this new jesus, this idea of Jesus. "There's no such thing as any new jesus. That ain't anything but a way to say something.… No such thing exists!" (*WB*, 158–59) Onnie Jay replies in disgust: "That's the trouble with you innerlekchuls, you don't never have nothing to show for what you're saying" (*WB*, 159). The "new jesus" is not real; it is just a way to say something.

When Enoch Emery shows Haze the shriveled bloodless mummy, presenting him as his amazing discovery of the new jesus who does not look like any other man, Haze is repulsed. This is not what he had in mind. He wants the new jesus to be clearly recognizable as a different kind of man, a man who looks better than any other man. And that is exactly what Onnie Jay Holy offers: an idea of Jesus, a new jesus who is more attractive than the old Jesus. But Haze realizes that both the mummy and the idea are lifeless and bloodless. He is compelled to deny that a new jesus really exists.

The idea and the mummy are the spiritual and the material, the highest and the lowest, completely separated and thus distorted. The mummy is merely dust, the lowliest dust of the earth from which God created Adam. O'Connor says that the mummy is "what man looks like without God" (*CW*, 920). The idea is the spiritualization of the incarnation. It is nothing more than an invention of the human mind, a new man who looks better than real men of flesh and blood. The new man of Haze's new church is free from original sin and is his own redeemer. As Haze's double, Onnie Jay's preacher, announces: "the unredeemed are redeeming theirselves." The idea and the mummy together do not make a whole man for both are lifeless and bloodless.

Enoch and Onnie Jay reveal the division within Haze himself, the division between his mind and his blood. Onnie Jay describes Haze as an "innerleckchul" because he sees that what Haze is looking for must be an idea, an abstraction. But Haze, like Enoch, has wise blood: his mind wants a new jesus, but his blood is too wise to accept anything less than the real Jesus. He seems to have inherited his obsession with Jesus from his grandfather, a "waspish" preacher with "Jesus hidden in his head like a stinger" (*WB*, 14). His grandfather says of his sinful grandson: "that boy had been redeemed and Jesus wasn't going to leave him ever" (*WB*, 16).

His grandfather's waspish preaching had stung Haze to the core: "There was already a deep black wordless conviction in him that the way to avoid Jesus was to avoid sin. He knew by the time he was twelve years old that he was going to be a preacher. Later he saw Jesus move from tree to tree in the back of his mind, a wild ragged figure motioning him to turn around and come off into the dark where he was not sure of his footing, where he might be walking on the water and not know it and then suddenly know it and drown" (*WB*, 16). Haze somehow understands what is at stake if he does turn around and go off into the dark, and he does not want to do it.

Three of the characters in *Wise Blood* recognize Haze's prophetic obsession with Jesus. Enoch tells him: "I knew when I first seen you you don't have nobody nor nothing but Jesus" (*WB*, 54). Even the fake blind preacher tells him: "You can't run away from Jesus. Jesus is a fact.... Some preacher has left his mark on you" (*WB*, 47). Sabbath Lily screams at him: "You didn't want nothing but Jesus!" Haze answers: "I don't want nothing but the truth!" (*WB*, 188) His single-minded pursuit of truth and his all-consuming desire for Jesus was somehow always there in spite of the fact that he wants to deny it. The conflict within him is a conflict between his inherited instinct and his mind. The tradition inherited from his grandfather is present in him as an instinct that he cannot ignore, as a rule and measure preventing him from accepting anything less than the true Jesus.

In showing us Haze's relentless drive to his ultimate end, O'Connor captures the meaning of Pascal's searching mind and the assurance from Christ: "You would not seek me if you had not found Me" (*P*, #919). The action displayed for our contemplation in *Wise Blood*, the action of grace, can be understood as the movement of Hazel Motes from this new jesus of his own invention to the historical reality of the incarnation and the redemptive power of the blood of Christ.

Haze was convinced that the way to avoid Jesus was to avoid sin. But the change that occurs in him is his growing recognition of the reality of original sin, the reality denied in Onnie Jay's idea of the new jesus. As O'Connor tells us, grace itself cannot be seen. It manifests itself in the changes that take place in the characters, expressed in both words and actions. In the first part of the story, Haze insists to Enoch: "I AM clean" (*WB*, 87). At the end of the story, in response to his landlady's shock at his extreme penitential practices, he explains: "I'm not clean" (*WB*, 228).

Haze is instinctually aware of the mystery of original sin, in spite of his determination to deny the reality of redemption: he could not escape "the nameless unplaced guilt that was in him" (*WB*, 59). Somehow he knows that, before there are sins, there is a first sin, a sinfulness that he did not choose: "If I was in sin I was in it before I ever committed any" (*WB*, 49). On one occasion, when Haze sees a sign on the side of the road that says: "WOE TO THE BLASPHEMER AND WHOREMONGER! WILL HELL SWALLOW YOU UP?", he responds: "There's no person a whoremonger, who wasn't something worse first. That's not the sin, nor blasphemy. The sin came before them" (*WB*, 72).

In his desperate search for truth, he concludes that there is no truth, a realization that forces upon him the essential displacement caused by original sin. "No truth behind all truths is what I and this church preach! Where you come from is gone, where you thought you were going to never was there, and where you are is no good unless you can get away from it. Where is there a place for you to be? No place. Nothing outside you can give you any place" (*WB*, 165). Later in the story, he makes explicit the source of this displacement in the fall of man and, in this recognition, he expresses the possibility of redemption. "In yourself right now is all the place you've got. If there was any Fall, look there, if there was any Redemption, look there, and if you expect any Judgment, look there, because they all three will have to be in your time and your body and where in your time and your body can they be? ... If there was a place where Jesus has redeemed you that would be the place for you to be" (*WB*, 166).

Without realizing it, Haze is actually truthful in his denials. For it is true both that redemption must occur in your time and your body and that the place for you to be is the place where Jesus has redeemed you. And that is exactly the place where Haze is headed.

After Haze takes the awful step of blinding himself, his landlady realizes something of what is going on beneath the surface. "To her, the blind man had the look of seeing something" (*WB*, 218). She believes that "he saw something that he couldn't get without being blind to everything else" (*WB*, 220). This is Haze's prophetic vision, penetrating the surface of things to the hidden mystery of Christ. O'Connor explains: "From my point of view Haze does not come into his absolute integrity until he blinds himself." His wise blood "gets him further and further inside himself where one may be supposed to find the answer," to find what one is really looking for. Wise blood "is something that enables you to go in the right direction after what you want." For Haze, the right direction is inward: "When Haze blinds himself he turns entirely to an inner vision" (*CW*, 920–21).

Because he has violently destroyed his own eyes (his opening to the reality of the visible world), his landlady could not make up her mind what would be inside his head and what would be outside his head. She could only imagine that the outside was inside: the whole world, "whatever was or had been or would be," must be inside his head. All place must be there. And with respect to time, she wonders: "How would he know if time was going backwards or forwards or if he was going with it?" Then, "she saw him going backwards to Bethlehem and she had to laugh" (*WB*, 222–23) for "time goes forward, it don't go backward" (*WB*, 232). Haze has found his time and place, in Bethlehem and within himself. He has reached that "peculiar crossroads where time and place and eternity somehow meet" (*MM*, 59). Haze has encountered the historical embodied reality of the incarnation. He knows he needs a flesh and blood redeemer.

To the modern mind, Haze's inability to get rid of the presence of Jesus from his mind is the unhealthy obsession destroying his life, one of those psychic dispositions inherited from his ancestors which must be overcome if he is to attain psychic health. The obsession creates a painful conflict within himself, preventing him from adjusting to the modern world. For O'Connor, however, Haze's internal conflict reveals the mystery of freedom embodied in the plot of *Wise Blood*: the mystery of freedom lies at a level deeper than the psychological.

In her Author's Note to *Wise Blood*, O'Connor writes that "Hazel Motes' integrity lies in his trying with such vigor to get rid of the ragged figure who moves from tree to tree in the back of his mind. For the author, Haze's integrity lies in his not being able to. Does one's integrity ever lie in what he is not able to do? I think that usually it does, for free will does not mean one will, but many wills conflicting in one man. Freedom cannot be conceived simply. It is a mystery and one which a novel, even a comic novel, can only be asked to deepen" (*WB*, 1). What Haze cannot deny is the historical reality of the incarnation. Integrity brings together his inherited instinct and his mind in the acceptance of the redeeming blood of Christ. Haze's path to redemption might be described as his embrace of the tradition which had always been there, bringing his mind into accord with the tradition that flows in his veins and recovering the Christian historical consciousness.

To the unhistorical consciousness of modern man, O'Connor opposes her "Christian Realism." The term "Christian Realism" has become necessary for her because "one of the awful things about writing when you are a Christian is that for you the ultimate reality is the Incarnation, the present reality is the Incarnation, and nobody believes in the Incarnation; that is, nobody in your audience." She insists: "I believe ... that there is only one Reality and that that is the end of it" (*HB*, 92).

In reply to Cecil Dawkins, who asked about the "missing link," the implicit standard of judgment which makes sense of everything in her stories, she writes:

> I don't really think the standard of judgment, the missing link, you spoke of that you find in my stories emerges from any religion but Christianity, because it concerns specifically Christ and the Incarnation, the fact that there has been *a unique intervention in history*. It's not a matter in these stories of Do Unto Others. That can be found in any ethical culture series. It is the fact of the Word made flesh. As The Misfit said, "He thrown everything off balance and it's nothing for you to do but follow Him or find some meanness." That is the fulcrum that lifts my particular stories. (*HB*, 226–27, emphasis added)

When The Misfit says that Jesus thrown everything off balance, "he is going to the very heart of the Christian mystery" (*Conv*, 112).

O'Connor's realism is guaranteed by Catholic dogma because dogma takes her out of her own mind to the mystery of the historical reality. She is not limited by her own "ideas" for she knows that she can see through the darkness of the familiar only in the light of the tradition. O'Connor insists that "dogma is the guardian of mystery" (*HB*, 365) and, therefore, "an instrument for penetrating reality. Christian dogma is about the only thing left in the world that surely guards and respects mystery" (*MM*, 178). The non-believer assumes that Christian tradition is a restriction and constraint on freedom of thought because it seems to him that the believer is obliged to accept certain doctrines that he does not really understand and to conform his vision of the world to those doctrines. O'Connor, however, argues that her faith actually allows her to see the world as it really is. "I have heard it said that belief in Christian doctrine is a hindrance to the writer, but I myself have found nothing further from the truth. Actually, it frees the story-teller to observe. It is not a set of rules which fixes what he sees in the world. It affects his writing primarily by guaranteeing his respect for mystery" (*MM*, 31). Her standard of judgment is the incarnation and the Christian mysteries which revolve around this central mystery. "I see from the standpoint of Christian orthodoxy. This means that for me the meaning of life is centered in our Redemption by Christ" (*MM*, 32).[11]

How does Christian doctrine free the story-teller to observe? It frees him from himself, from his illusions of his own completeness. The

---

11   William F. Lynch, *Christ and Apollo: The Dimensions of the Literary Imagination* (1960, repr. Belmont, NC: Wiseblood Books, 2021), 71. Lynch emphasizes this historical experience of Catholic doctrine: "Catholic doctrine is ... a divine command of the mind and the will to enter, on the divine and human planes, into an historical, actual and *eventful* set of facts which penetrate reality to the hilt.... The Creed begins with God and ends with eternal life for men, but in between is time, that time through which Christ passed and that time through which doctrine implicitly commands us to pass."

novelist "begins to see in the depths of himself, and it seems to me that his position there rests on what must certainly be the bedrock of all human experience—the experience of limitation or, if you will, poverty" (*MM*, 131–32). The integrity of the novelist consists in seeing himself as he really is: "In the process of making a novel, the serious novelist faces, in the most extreme way, his own limitations" (*MM*, 183).[12] The tradition frees the novelist from his own limited ideas because the tradition preserves the Christian mystery.

Christina Bieber Lake explains how the certitude of doctrine can actually free the writer from uncertainty about what he sees. "Stories have focus and perspective; since the writer without faith commitments must speak from *somewhere*, she ends up speaking according to personal whim. So it is, paradoxically, the Catholic fiction writer who is 'entirely free to observe' precisely because she has no freedom to invent her own values. Without the burden to remake the world, the committed

---

12   O'Connor's Christian realism must begin within herself. She follows the advice of the great French novelist Francois Mauriac: "purify the source" (*MM*, 149). The writer must first look within himself for he "begins to see in the depths of himself" (*MM*, 131–32). She explains that the writer "will have to descend far enough into himself to reach those underground springs that give life to his work.... It will be a descent through the darkness of the familiar" (*MM*, 50). O'Connor says that "the writer has to judge himself with a stranger's eye and a stranger's severity." The novelist must begin with an examination of conscience (*MM*, 130) and the only conscience he has to examine in this matter is his own (*MM*, 32). "The Christian writer will feel that in the greatest depth of vision, moral judgment will be implicit ... moral judgment is part of the very act of seeing" (*MM*, 30–31). Unlike the unhistorical consciousness which breaks with the moral standard of the tradition, O'Connor's judgment is fundamentally moral in the Christian sense. For O'Connor, judgment means that "the prophet in [her] has to see the freak" (*MM*, 81–82). However, to begin within oneself is not to reduce the work of art to the status of the self-expression of the artist: "No art is sunk in the self, but rather, in art the self becomes self-forgetful in order to meet the demands of the thing seen and the thing being made" (*MM*, 81–82).

writer can see it truly.... The Christian writer is never left only to his 'personal imaginative gift,' but has access to a whole history, a whole prophetic vision that he did not make."[13] Romano Guardini makes the crucial point: the church, as the bearer of authority, lifts the individual's relationship to Christ "out of the danger of subjectivity," which is the great danger for the modern mind.[14]

O'Connor describes Christian historical consciousness in the terms of Pascal's conversion experience. Of her own life, she says, "all my own experience has been that of the writer who believes, ... in Pascal's words, in the 'God of Abraham, Isaac, and Jacob and not of the philosophers and scholars'" (*MM*, 161). Jesus Christ *is* the God of Abraham, Isaac, and Jacob.

As Pascal insists, classical philosophy, medieval natural theology, and above all, modern philosophy cannot provide an adequate account of the relationship between the human being and the divine being who becomes a man, enters human history, and dies for our salvation. Because these world-changing events have actually occurred, a new approach must be taken. As O'Connor says through The Misfit, Jesus "thrown everything off balance" (*HB*, 227).

In his essay on the *Pensées*, T. S. Eliot describes Pascal's approach to the recovery of the reality of the incarnation for the modern mind. Pascal looks at the world, especially at the moral world within. "He finds its character inexplicable by any non-religious theory: among religions he finds Christianity, and Catholic Christianity, to account most satisfactorily" for what he sees; "and thus, by ... 'powerful and concurrent' reasons, he finds himself inexorably committed to the dogma of the Incarnation."[15] Pascal does not begin from faith as the theologians do; he does not begin from nature as the classical philosophers do; he does not begin from reflection on the

---

13   Lake, *Incarnational Art*, 144–45.
14   Guardini, *Pascal*, 191.
15   Eliot, "The *Pensées* of Pascal," 360.

mind as modern philosophers do. Rather, he begins from the moral human condition. This is Pascal's "true philosophy" which looks at the moral world unblinkingly, considers all of the available explanations for moral failure, and is open to the possibility that there has been a divine revelation of the mystery which alone makes it possible for us to understand ourselves in our fallen condition.

Pascal's approach to the historical reality of the incarnation, as it is articulated in response to modern philosophy and to Montaigne's skepticism in particular, provides us with a deeper understanding of the meaning of O'Connor's Christian Realism.

Pascal's most extensive discussion of Montaigne is found in the record of a conversation in which he presents his views on Epictetus and Montaigne as representative of philosophical dogmatism and skepticism respectively. Pascal is recorded as saying of Montaigne that, "since he was born in a Christian state, he professed the Catholic faith, and there is nothing unusual about that. But since he wished to determine what moral reason should dictate without the light of faith, he based his principles on that supposition, and so, considering man devoid of all revelation, he discoursed in that vein." (*SW*, 124). Montaigne wants to free man from the authority of revelation and, therefore, he "is absolutely pernicious to those who are inclined to impiety and to vice" (*SW*, 132).

Montaigne's spiritualization of the incarnation will be discussed more fully in chapter 2. Here, I address the first step towards this spiritualization, that is, the liberation of man from the authority of divine revelation through the reduction of sacred tradition to mere pious custom. By reducing Christianity to mere custom, Montaigne rejects the divine origin and authority of sacred tradition.

In reply to those who claim that Christian faith is brought about in the believer "by a particular inspiration of divine grace" (*E*, 321), Montaigne argues that we are Christians because we happen to have been born in a country where Christianity was in practice. "We are Christians by the same title that we are Perigordians or Germans" (*E*, 325). He may observe its practices outwardly, but he does not see tradition the way a believer sees it: he looks at Christianity not as a participant in the practice of faith but as a detached observer of the variety of religious custom.

In his confrontation with Montaigne, Pascal accepts as his starting point Montaigne's modern skeptical stance toward Christianity. That is, Pascal begins, not by assuming the truth of Christianity, but by looking at Christianity as just one religion among many. In a fragment which refers explicitly to Montaigne's most skeptical essay ("The Apology for Sebond"), Pascal presents Montaigne's position that all religions are essentially the same for they all have ceremonies, teachings, and practices. Pascal answers: "If you hardly care about knowing the truth, that is enough to leave you in peace, but if you desire with all your heart to know it, you have not looked closely enough at the details. This would do for a philosophical question, but here where everything is at stake …" (*P*, #150).

Pascal moves beyond the initial stance of disinterested observer of Christianity among all other religions by finding the truth of Christianity in its uniqueness among all religions. Montaigne's reduction of tradition to custom makes no distinction between the essential core and the accidental features of the tradition. Taking the approach of reducing all religions to custom because they have similar beliefs and practices shows that "you hardly care about knowing the truth." Pascal writes: "the true source of truth … is tradition" (*P*, #865). He asserts this Catholic position in the aftermath of the Protestant Reformation which rejected the authority of tradition. Sacred tradition has its great power and authority because it begins by a divine transmission.[16] Tradition is not a human invention or creation: it has a divine origin and the truth that it carries is uncreated truth.[17]

---

[16] Yves Congar, OP, *The Meaning of Tradition*, trans. A. N. Woodrow (San Francisco: Ignatius Press, 2004), 10.

[17] Congar, 69.

Pascal's recovery of the core of the tradition in the historical reality of the incarnation is central to his confrontation with modern consciousness and its spiritualization of the incarnation. Romano Guardini formulates Pascal's unequivocal response to the unhistorical consciousness and its spiritualization of the incarnation: "There is no 'essence of Christianity' separable from [Christ]—we repeat, separable from him, and expressible in a free-floating conceptual scheme. The essence of Christianity is Christ.... A demand is here made of the philosophical mind, which is, in reality, a stumbling block for mere philosophy: that the definitive category of Christianity ... is the particular, unique reality of the concrete personality of Jesus of Nazareth."[18]

The historical reality of the divinity of Christ is a "scandal" for the philosophical mind because a merely historical reality is too lowly to satisfy the mind's desire for a universal and disembodied essence, too lowly for the mind's desire for the absolute. The God of Abraham, Isaac, and Jacob is not reached by an ascent of thought, but rather through historical revelation. He is the God "of those men ... who lived at a given time, in a given country, in a definitely localized attitude, in a specifiable historical context. But it is 'scandal and folly' for the mind enclosed in its philosophy to be obliged to acquiesce in this apparently arbitrary binding of the absolute to historical contingency."[19]

Pascal identifies three ways in which Christianity is unique among all religions in its faith in the historical reality of the incarnation. These three unique beliefs are central to O'Connor's Christian Realism.

First, *"That God wished to hide himself.* If there were only one religion, God would be clearly manifest. If there were no martyrs except in our religion, likewise. God being thus hidden, any religion that does not say that God is hidden is not true, and any religion which does not explain

---

18   Guardini, *Pascal*, 40.
19   Guardini, 39.

why does not instruct. Ours does all this. *Verily thou art a God that hidest thyself*" (P, #242). Christianity explains why the God of revelation is a hidden God.

The god of the philosophers is the god of Aristotle, manifested in the visible order of the universe, the god who makes sense of the natural world. The God of Abraham, Isaac, and Jacob is Jesus Christ, the hidden God, hidden in the incarnation yet revealing the incomprehensible mystery of our redemption. It is both "impossible [and] useless to know God without Christ" (P, #191). Pascal writes: "If the world existed in order to teach man about God, his Divinity would shine out on every hand in a way that could not be gainsaid; but as it only exists through Christ, for Christ, and to teach men about their corruption and redemption, everything in it blazes with proofs of these two truths. What can be seen on earth indicates neither the total absence, nor the manifest presence of divinity, but the presence of a hidden God. Everything bears this stamp" (P, #449).

Pascal's insistence on the hiddenness of the divinity leads us deeper and deeper into the full force of the reality of this mystery. The God of Abraham, Isaac, and Jacob remained hidden "under the veil of nature which hid him from us until the Incarnation." Yet, when he finally did appear, he did so under another veil, the veil of human flesh, and was thus hidden even more than before. "He was far more recognizable when he was invisible than when he had rendered himself visible." It is more difficult to recognize the divinity of Christ than to find God in nature, for Christ reveals the true being of the hidden God in a way that nature cannot. Hidden in human flesh, his glory and power are more invisible, for he humbled himself in coming among men with no outward difference.

Finally, he chose to remain among us "in the strangest and most hidden mystery of all," in the Eucharist. "This is the sacrament which in the Apocalypse Saint John calls a hidden manna. And I believe Isaiah saw it in this state when he said in the spirit of prophecy: 'Verily, thou art a hidden God.' That is the final secret in which he may be.... To recognize him through the species of bread is the attribute of Catholics alone" (*SW*, 146–47). The incarnation and the Eucharist both hide and reveal the historical and embodied presence of Christ in the world. "Just as Jesus remained unknown among men, so the truth remains among popular opinions with no outward difference. Thus the Eucharist and ordinary bread" (*P*, #225). Christ is hidden in the most ordinary and familiar.

The second way in which Pascal presents the uniqueness of Christianity is through the role of prophetic vision: "I see a number of religions in conflict, and therefore all false, except one. Each of them wishes to be believed on its own authority and threatens unbelievers. I do not believe them on that account. Anyone can say that. Anyone can call himself a prophet, but I see Christianity, and find its prophecies, which are not something that anyone can do" (*P*, #198).

The very existence and meaning of the prophetic tradition affirm the historical reality of the Christian mystery. The God of the prophets is the God of Abraham, Isaac, and Jacob, the divine eternal being who entered human history. While Montaigne reduces tradition to mere custom by tracing tradition back to an origin in time so that it appears arbitrary, accidental, and weak, and thus loses its authority over our minds, Pascal shows us the foundation of the tradition in the eternal. "The Messiah has always been believed in. The tradition of Adam was still fresh in Noah and Moses.... Thus with the fulfillment of the prophecies the Messiah has been proved forever" (*P*, #282). Christianity is radically new in the history of mankind. But it is really the manifestation of what was always already there: "it has always existed on earth [for] Christ [was] promised since the world began.... The Church ... worships him who has always been" (*P*, #281).

The eternity of the tradition proves the divinity of the true religion: "the fact that this religion has always been preserved inflexibly shows that it is divine" (*P*, #280). Pascal establishes the authority of the tradition on its eternity. "There is always the overriding principle of tradition, of the faith of the ancient Church" (*P*, #285), for "our religion is divine in the Gospel, the Apostles and tradition" (*P*, #287). The Christian historical consciousness (which is, in the deepest sense, the tradition) is grounded in the eternal incarnate truth.

Finally, Pascal identifies the uniqueness of Christianity as the demand for hatred of oneself and faith in a humiliated God: "No other religion has proposed that we should hate ourselves. No other religion therefore can please those who hate themselves and seek a being who is worthy of love. And if they had never [before] heard of the religion of a humiliated God, they would at once embrace it" (*P*, #220). Christianity is the religion of a humiliated God, the divine eternal being who took on our humanity and entered human history to shed his blood and die an ignominious death on the cross for our salvation. The divinity is hidden in the humiliated redeemer. That is the compelling argument for the truth of the Christian religion.

The tradition must be *recovered* for the modern mind from its reduction to mere custom. The tradition must become astonishing, and it must become astonishing through the revelation of the core of the tradition as the hidden, humiliated God, hidden in his humiliation, his lowliness, among the common and lowly. Jesus remained unknown among men because there is no "outward" difference. What, then, is the "inner" hidden difference? The difference is the lowliness—the freely chosen lowliness—of Christ. That is what makes the recovery of the incarnation astonishing, finding the divinity where we did not expect it, because we were looking for something better, something "spiritual."

In recovering the core of the tradition in the historical embodied reality of the incarnation, Pascal stands against the spiritualization of the incarnation at the heart of philosophical modernity. O'Connor recovers that same reality in her stories. When all is said and done, O'Connor's prophet-freaks cannot deny the unique historical intervention on which everything depends and which demands everything of us. Hazel Motes is a modern man looking for a new jesus who looks better than the humiliated Jesus who shed his blood. But this new jesus could only be an idea, an idol of human making. Behind Haze's denials of the new jesus is the dawning realization that, as Pascal says, Jesus is hidden among other men with no outward difference. He looks just like any other man. Only the eyes of faith can recognize him. In the violent act of blinding himself, Haze smashes the idols of spiritualization. "If your eye has caused you to sin, tear it out and throw it away" (Matthew 18:9). Only now can the blind prophet Hazel see the real Jesus, the child in the manger in Bethlehem.

2. Hulga's Heart Condition: The Disembodied and Detached Modern Mind

O'Connor captures the essence of the truly modern man in a comic image. In *Wise Blood*, she describes a movie that Enoch Emery went to see. The movie was about "a scientist named The Eye who performed operations by remote control. You would wake up in the morning and find a slit in your chest or head or stomach and something you couldn't do without would be gone" (*WB*, 138). Within himself, the modern man is the scientific observer (the Eye) and the hollowed out human being. What has been emptied out is the "heart."

O'Connor displays this new modern individual in her portraits of Rayber in *The Violent Bear It Away* and of Hulga in "Good Country People." Rayber is a psychologist; Hulga has a doctorate in philosophy. Both, then, are highly educated and deliberate in their embrace of the modern ethos. The character of Rayber will be discussed in chapter 3. In this chapter, I focus on Hulga in order to bring out more clearly O'Connor's profound insight into the detachment and disembodiment of the modern mind, and the meaning of this detachment and disembodiment for human life.

Hulga is a thirty-two-year-old woman who lives with her mother because her heart condition prevents her from working as a philosophy professor. On account of an accident with a shotgun, Hulga has a wooden leg, which she treats with a kind of reverence and secrecy. She has changed her name from *Joy* to the ugly name *Hulga*, and her chosen name is "her highest creative act" because, in that act, she has rejected her mother, her natural origin, for her own power of self-creation: "One of her major triumphs was that her mother had not been able to turn her dust into Joy, but the greater one was that she had been able to turn it herself into Hulga" (*CS*, 275). Hulga's disposition is one of "constant outrage" which has "obliterated every expression from her face" (*CS*, 273).

Hulga regards herself as much superior to her mother and to the uneducated people who surround her because, as an atheist and a nihilist, she has no illusions: "I don't have illusions. I'm one of those people who see *through* to nothing" (*CS*, 287). When a young Bible salesman comes to the house, Hulga decides that it would be interesting—a kind of experiment—to try to seduce him. Assuming that the young man was an innocent simpleton, she thought about how she would have to reckon with his remorse: "True genius can get an idea across even to an inferior mind. She imagined that she took his remorse in hand and changed it into a deeper understanding of life. She took all his shame away and turned it into something useful" (*CS*, 284). This deeper understanding of life, then, is an "idea."

Proceeding with her experiment, Hulga leads the young man on until he kisses her. "The kiss, which had more pressure than feeling behind it, produced that extra surge of adrenalin in the girl that enables one to carry a pack trunk out of a burning house, but in her, the power went at once to the brain. Even before he released her, her mind, clear and detached and ironic anyway, was regarding him from a great distance, with amusement but with pity. She had never been kissed before and she was pleased to discover that it was an unexceptional experience and all a matter of the mind's control" (*CS*, 285).

Hulga pities the subject of her experiment. As their kissing becomes more intense, he asks her if she loves him, insisting that she must say that she loves him, but Hulga is most reluctant to use the term *love*. At one point, she looks at him almost tenderly. "You poor baby. It's just as well you don't understand.... We are all damned, but some of us have taken off our blindfolds and see that there's nothing to see. It's a kind of salvation" (*CS*, 287–88). It turns out, of course, that the Bible salesman is not at all innocent and it is Hulga who is seduced. The Bible salesman is interested in her only because of her wooden leg. As he runs off with the artificial leg, he calls out: "you ain't so smart. I been believing in nothing ever since I was born" (*CS*, 291).

O'Connor explains how Hulga's wooden leg accumulates meaning in this story. "Early in the story, we're presented with the fact that the Ph.D. is spiritually as well as physically crippled. She believes in nothing but her own belief in nothing, and we perceive that there is a wooden part of her soul that corresponds to her wooden leg.... And when the Bible salesman steals it, the reader realizes that he has taken away part of the girl's personality and has revealed her deeper affliction to her for the first time" (*MM*, 99). The story builds up to "her realization in the end that she ain't so smart," the moment of grace in which Hulga begins to see herself as she really is, in her "pride of intellect" (*HB*, 170). The image of the wooden leg captures the condition of the personality in the grip of modern consciousness: something essentially human is missing.

In the scene in which Hulga and the young man kiss, O'Connor presents us with a perfect description of the modern philosopher and modern consciousness. Instead of being caught up in the passion of the kiss, Hulga is observing herself. Hulga's mind is "detached" from her body and from what she is doing. She looks at the young man "from a great distance," detached from him and the activity in which she is engaged with him. She sees the kiss as affecting something from which she herself is separated, her own body as it is being changed: she is observing her own reactions to a merely physical act in which she is not really participating.

Hulga is detached, unfeeling, and "sees through" the experience, pleased with the realization that a kiss is nothing exceptional. The kiss is reduced to a physical pressure of the lips, and its effect is an experience of a merely biological surge of adrenalin, the power of which goes immediately to her brain. She is the detached observer of what is happening to her. She cannot be moved because *experience* is reduced to observation of her own body as it reacts to the touch of the young man's lips. This "objective" observation is the stance of the modern scientist. Hulga sees through everything to nothing: the kiss is unexceptional because it is "all a matter of the mind's control." Experience has no meaning for her because she cannot experience what she can't control. Reality cannot astound her, shock her, bring her up short, because *seeing through* means abstracting out only what the mind can control, stripping away anything mysterious. Control means reducing all action to merely physical motion and change. For Hulga, experience is *experiment*.

Hulga wants to see what the kiss is. But you cannot see what human action really is when you are the detached observer. Seeing *objectively* is not seeing it *as it is in itself* because seeing objectively means reducing it to physical motion and change. Human action is reduced to *behavior*. The only way to see human action as it is in itself is to participate in it. *Experience* is participation and action, not merely observing something that *happens* to you but understanding something you are doing. Hulga is touched, literally and physically, in the kiss. But she is not affected—not touched in her very being—because she is not really participating but only observing herself.

O'Connor is showing us the distortion of human being in modern consciousness. Humanness as such is identified with the detached mind. In this separation of the mind from the body, what is lost is the heart, the affective capacity of the human being to be open to and moved by reality. For Hulga, everything becomes ordinary because nothing touches her heart, her affective capacity through which she might be moved and respond to something outside herself. Her heart is anesthetized, suppressed in the determination to control rather than be open to the unexpected and unknown and to be changed by it at the deepest level of her being.

The meaning of Hulga's modern consciousness can be brought out more fully when we see it emerge in early modern philosophy in the *Essays* of Montaigne and then develop in the psychology of Jung where this radically new understanding of human being forms the basis of the psychoanalytic ethos which O'Connor finds so pervasive in her audience. Pascal's insistence on the centrality of the "heart" for human existence will then be shown to be essential to his response to Montaigne and his critique of modern philosophy. Hulga's "heart condition" is O'Connor's dramatic portrayal of the distortion of human consciousness in the modern world.

Montaigne makes a radical break with the pre-modern experience of the mind. In the classical-Christian tradition of the pre-modern world, the mind is not experienced as detached and disembodied, for the mind is essentially embodied, its activities grounded in the bodily senses. The human being understands himself as an animal within nature, an animal who is higher than all other animals because he can think: he is the animal with the *logos* or the rational animal. Drawn out by wonder to know the whole of all that is, the pre-modern philosopher is absorbed in the contemplation of being, of God, and of nature (the subject matter of metaphysics and physics). The mind is naturally and essentially receptive: it knows itself only indirectly, in its activity of grasping the intelligibility of things. The pre-modern mind, then, is not immediately conscious of itself but loses itself in the object of contemplation.

In contrast to this natural direction of the mind to the world, Montaigne's modern consciousness is *self*-consciousness. Self-consciousness is achieved in the modern philosophical act of "reflection." Instead of being aware of itself indirectly as engaged with the world and with God, the self-conscious mind turns back on itself and becomes aware of itself. This philosophical act of the reflection of the mind on itself is the origin of modern philosophy.[1]

Montaigne's stance on himself in the *Essays* is precisely this reflexive action of self-consciousness: "I study myself more than any other subject. That is my metaphysics, that is my physics" (*E*, 821). Reflection means a

---

1   O'Connor points explicitly to the relevance of modern philosophical reflection for her portrait of Hulga in her reference to the philosopher Nicolas Malebranche (1638–1715). In a moment of exasperation with her unreflective, opinionated mother, Hulga blurts out: "Woman! do you ever look inside? Do you ever look inside and see what you are *not*? God! ... Malebranche was right: we are not our own light. We are not our own light!" (*CS*, 276). Hulga is exasperated because her mother is incapable of reflecting on her own mind. See Nicolas Malebranche, *Dialogues on Metaphysics and on Religion*, ed. Nicholas Jolley, trans. David Scott (Cambridge: Cambridge University Press, 1997), Dialogue III, 32–33. However, Hulga believes that she herself is indeed her own light for she is a modern philosopher who believes neither in God nor in the createdness of the world. She sees by her own light and so she sees through everything to the meaninglessness of everything. There is nothing which has inherent value for her except her own power of vision which eliminates all mystery from human life. Henry T. Edmondson III, in "'Wingless Chickens': 'Good Country People' and the Seduction of Nihilism," *Flannery O'Connor Review* 2 (2003): 70, explains Hulga's nihilism in terms of Descartes's method of doubt and the Cartesian scientific method. He argues that Malebranche's attempt to prove the truth of the religious tradition by means of human reason cannot succeed. Malebranche "promoted Descartes's divorce of mind and matter," but he did so under the cover of religion. "Malebranche was opposed by Pascal ... who realized that much of the mystery of human nature was simply not amenable to rational resolution in the manner by which a problem of physics might yield to analysis." In his *Return to Good and Evil: Flannery O'Connor's Response to Nihilism* (Lanham, MD: Lexington Books, 2002), 24, Edmondson focuses on Nietzsche's nihilism and his disdain for "the herd" and admiration for the overman whose task is "to overturn Western moral values and create something new." This is the disdain that we see in Hulga's attitude toward those she believes are her intellectual inferiors and in her plan to transform the Bible salesman's remorse into something useful.

"doubling" of the mind so that the mind gets outside itself, as it were, and then turns back to itself and observes itself. This separation is effected by an act of "detachment" from oneself: "I dare not only to speak of myself, but to speak only of myself; I go astray when I write of anything else, and get away from my subject. I do not love myself so indiscriminately, nor am I so attached and wedded to myself, that I cannot distinguish and consider myself apart, as I do a neighbor or a tree" (*E*, 720). Montaigne can look at himself as if he is a stranger to himself. His detachment allows him to *spy* on himself: "each man is a good education to himself, provided he has the capacity to spy on himself from close up" (*E*, 272). Detachment and spying are the separation of the detached mind from the natural man and the observation of the natural man by the detached mind. That is precisely Hulga's experience in the act of kissing the Bible salesman.

One of the clearest examples of Montaigne's detachment and spying occurs in his essay "Of practice," where he recounts the incident in which he came so close to death that he was shown "the face and the idea of death" (*E*, 269). In a violent collision with a large and powerful horse, he had been thrown from his own horse and was unconscious, bleeding, and almost dead. His description of his return to consciousness presents him as if he were hovering over himself, watching himself, observing his natural faculties as they re-awaken. He spies on himself as if he were a stranger: he watches what is happening to himself.

Pierre Manent explains Montaigne's doubling of himself and spying on himself in this incident of observing himself coming back from the dead. In Montaigne, Manent sees the profound transformation of the consciousness of the human being from active participant in the world to the "objective observer-passive subject" of modern self-consciousness.[2] Self-consciousness is the consciousness of the objective observer-passive subject.

---

2   Pierre Manent, *Montaigne: Life without Law*, trans. Paul Seaton (Notre Dame, IN: Notre Dame University Press, 2020), 117.

Manent explains how the objective observer-passive subject comes into existence. The agent in Montaigne was "deactivated," and made available for "objective knowledge." What it means to say that the agent is "de-activated" is that he no longer "acts" but merely "undergoes." The passive subject, the subject of observation, is like a corpse, a body that cannot act but is merely subject to change. Montaigne looks at what the natural man is doing as if he himself is not the originator of those movements of his soul, but is simply undergoing what is happening in himself.

Turning the natural man into something passive means choosing to see all movement, all change in the subject, not as intended, not as the free action initiated by the human being, but as merely change that he undergoes. As we will see in our discussion of Jung, Jungian psychoanalytic practice relies heavily on the interpretation of dreams because dreams simply happen to us. "The dream gives a true picture of the subjective state," for the dream is "the expression of an involuntary psychic process not controlled by the conscious outlook. *It presents the subjective state as it really is*" (*MMSS*, 5, emphasis added).

In order to see himself objectively, the human being must become the passive subject. Objective and subjective are counterparts: the kind of knowledge which is objective requires a passive subject. In other words, the only way to have objective knowledge is to turn nature (including human nature) into something passive, because the subject that is passive can be controlled and changed at will. Objective knowledge, then, is for the sake of control and power. A passive nature is a malleable, changeable nature.

Montaigne, the modern man, is not satisfied with his given nature. So, he must do better than creation. He must, through his own self-consciousness, become his own creator, rebelling against the God who has given him, without his consent, the nature that he is burdened with. Gerhard Kruger explains that "reflection in the fundamental, philosophical sense of the word, man's 'reflectivity', presupposes *the powerlessness of man before God*, as it is understood by Christianity."[3] Therefore, "self-consciousness forms itself *in defiance of* all divine omnipotence."[4]

Montaigne's act of self-consciousness is presented in terms of the Christian mystery of dying to oneself, of death and resurrection, accomplished through his own power. He "dies to himself" and is resurrected as the new man, the self-conscious being who is the detached observer-passive subject of philosophical reflection and modern consciousness. Thus, the true meaning of the incarnation, of the mystery of redemption, becomes the human achievement of the self-consciousness of modern man. Montaigne's own self-understanding, then, is his abstraction of this purely human meaning from the embodied historical reality of the Christian mystery. In this spiritualization of the incarnation, Christianity is subjected to modern philosophy for the purpose of making man his own master, his own creator and redeemer.

How are we to grasp the meaning of the modern detached and disembodied mind in concrete terms? Montaigne's description of his encounter with death—his mind hovering over his body as he watches his natural faculties return—is an image of the new modern man. The image is a representation of the new *stance* that the modern man takes on himself, the way he regards himself. Instead of actively participating, losing himself and fully engaging himself in his actions, the reflective individual is always looking at himself as he undergoes what happens to him. That is precisely what we see in Hulga's experience as she kisses the Bible salesman.

In concrete terms, this detached and disembodied mind is the mind of the modern scientist. Perhaps the last thing that a reader of Montaigne would conclude is that the *Essays* display a scientific mind. On the contrary, the wandering, whimsical, accidental flow

---

3 Gerhard Kruger, "The Origin of Philosophical Self-Consciousness," trans. Fabrice Paradis Beland, *New Yearbook for Phenomenology and Phenomenological Philosophy* 7 (2007): 215.

4 Kruger, 231.

of his thought, the absence of rigorous scientific proof, the pervasive self-centeredness of his focus, all suggest what we might describe as his "subjective" orientation. But that is the point. The *stance* that he takes on himself, the place where he stands to see himself, is the stance of the detached observer. He is observing this subjectivity, and he is observing it in a particular way: the scientific method ensures his "objectivity." The method of observation is not the natural receptive procedure of the natural intellect as it observes what it seeks to understand, for the scientific method does not allow the mind to simply follow its own natural course. As Francis Bacon writes of the new science: "The whole operation of the mind must be completely re-started, so that from the very beginning it is not left to itself, but is always subject to rule."[5] Modern science proceeds by the method of experiment.

The title that Montaigne chooses for his work, *Essays*, carries the meaning of *experiments*. In *The Kingdom of Man: Genesis and Failure of the Modern Project*, Remi Brague notes that the beginning of the period that we call "modern" is marked by "an increased prevalence of words that designate 'essay,' 'attempt,' 'experience' in the sense of 'experiment.'"[6] Brague claims that this is most evident in Montaigne's *Essays*, the experiment with himself that is his modern project.

Hulga's attempt to seduce the Bible salesman is an experiment. She wants to observe herself as undergoing the encounter, reflecting on its effects on her. She wants to observe her effect on him, getting him to do what she wants him to do, and then changing his shame into something useful for his improvement. The experiment is the invention of modern science. It is the way in which the detachment and spying of the observer operate in modern science. The scientist abandons the natural attitude toward the world and adopts the stance of the detached and disembodied mind.

---

[5] Francis Bacon, *Novum Organum*, trans. Peter Urbach and John Gibson (Chicago: Open Court, 1994), 38.

[6] Remi Brague, *The Kingdom of Man: Genesis and Failure of the Modern Project*, trans. Paul Seaton (Notre Dame, IN: University of Notre Dame Press, 2018), 2.

The experiment introduces a new level of distance, of separation, between the mind and the experience we have of the world in our everyday encounters with it. As Bacon explains: "simple experience …, if taken as it comes, is called accident; if it is deliberately sought, it is called experiment."[7] The experiment is a "deliberately sought" experience, a highly structured and controlled event of observation in order to see what happens.[8]

The *Essays* are the trials and tests of the natural mind, the "deliberately sought" experience of the natural mind by the detached observer, the natural mind put to the test by the detached observer. Montaigne performs what had seemed to be the impossible task of the mind looking at itself. To "deliberately seek" an experience of the natural mind is to double the mind, bringing the detached observer into being. In the *Essays* we are catching a glimpse of the detached observer coming into being in the stance that Montaigne takes on himself. This is also Hulga's stance on herself.

Modern natural science, the social sciences, and empirical psychology are all manifestations of the stance of the detached observer. Perhaps the clearest example of the phenomenon of the detached observer-passive subject is the science of psychiatry: the scientific mind of the psychiatrist uncovering the hidden "unconscious" motives of the patient. The modern man tends to see himself as the subject of psychiatry, to understand himself in the terms of the science of psychology. While this self-consciousness is especially evident in the highly educated, it is also present now throughout the culture. We can see this in the way we so easily give psychological reasons for our actions and feelings and the way we so

---

7   Bacon, *Novum Organum*, 91.

8   In other words, reflection is very different from what we might call "introspection." Introspection is the attempt to observe oneself in action. Self-consciousness, on the contrary, requires the deactivation of the acting human being so that the objective observer can see what happens. By the standards of modern science, natural introspection is haphazard and subjective, not controlled and objective. The natural mind cannot see itself "objectively."

readily accept such reasons as adequate explanations of human conduct. Evil, for example, is explained away as mental illness.

O'Connor confronts this pervasive modern consciousness in the work of the psychiatrist Carl Gustav Jung. David Z. Wehner explains that "O'Connor saw Jung as more dangerous than Freud because, whereas Freud at least tried to demarcate a clear line between science and religion, Jung enthusiastically erased such a line, believing that psychoanalysis could complement a religion that no longer addressed modernity's psychic needs."[9] The years during which O'Connor published her work were the "golden age" of the popularization of psychoanalysis in America. Psychoanalysis was the new religion, with the analyst as priest, uncondemning listener, and surgeon of the soul.[10] According to Wehner, "Jung believed the psychotherapist provides what the rituals and imagery of the church once did: a method for managing and encountering 'the unaccountable forces' of the collective unconscious."[11]

My discussion of Jung's psychology is not an attempt to present his thought in its entirety. I focus only on the works that O'Connor herself read and commented on: *Modern Man in Search of a Soul* and *The Undiscovered Self*, the two works of Jung that were in her library.[12] Further, it must be emphasized that even if Jung's practice of psychoanalysis is out of fashion among psychiatrists and psychologists, the stance of the human being in psychoanalysis is not peculiar to Jungian psychoanalysis but is fundamental to the phenomenon of modern consciousness as such.

In the posture of psychoanalysis, the human being becomes the self-conscious detached observer-passive subject. Jung says that the

---

9 David Z. Wehner, "Pulverizing the Idols: Flannery O'Connor's Battle with Sigmund Freud and Carl Jung," *The Mississippi Quarterly* 65, no. 2 (Spring 2012): 300.
10 Wehner, 303.
11 Wehner, 303. For an excellent discussion of Jung's reception by religious authors, see Barry Ulanov, *Jung and the Outside World*, chapter 3.
12 Wehner, "Pulverizing Idols," 299.

psychoanalyst is the "scientific observer" (*MMSS*, 26). The "scientific objectivity" of the doctor "enables him to see his patient not only as a human being but also as a subhuman who is bound to his body, like an animal" (*US*, 76). In the process of psychoanalysis, the patient is supposed to gradually assume this posture of scientific objectivity within himself, becoming within himself the objective observer-passive subject, thus becoming *self*-conscious.

The task of the analyst is "widening the consciousness" of the patient by "the procedure of bringing to light the parts of the personality which were previously unconscious and subjecting them to conscious discrimination and criticism" (*MMSS*, 10). Nowhere is this procedure more clearly demonstrated than in the analysis of dreams: the dream gives a true picture of the subjective state, because the dream is "the expression of an involuntary psychic process not controlled by the conscious outlook. *It presents the subjective state as it really is*" (*MMSS*, 5, emphasis added). Because "dreams are the direct expression of unconscious psychic activity," they throw light on "the unconscious causal factors" of the patient's trouble. The realm of the unconscious consists of the impulses, instincts, and feelings, such as depression, fear, anxiety, and shame, which are painful to undergo. Through the method of psychoanalysis, the therapist helps the patient to uncover the causes of these psychic events, explains them to the patient, thus freeing him from their troublesome effects (*MMSS*, 2).

The passive subject, then, experiences psychic activity, not as something he does, but as something he undergoes: "The dream content is to be taken in all seriousness as something that has actually happened to us; it should be treated as a contributory factor in framing our conscious outlook" (*MMSS*, 18). Dreams and other forms of psychic activity are *real*. "Dreams give information about the secrets of the inner life and reveal to the dreamer hidden factors of his personality." When these factors are hidden, unconscious, they cause disturbances and symptoms in waking life. "We cannot effectively treat the patient from the side of consciousness alone, but must bring about a change in and through the unconscious" (*MMSS*, 16).

In the relationship between doctor and patient, there is an interplay of objectivity and subjectivity with the patient himself becoming more and more objective (*US*, 51–52). Progress is made as the patient becomes increasingly capable of bringing his own psychic activity to light, making it conscious, and submitting it to analysis himself. In other words, he becomes more active, taking a greater role in the widening of his consciousness, and becoming more self-conscious. Jung says that his purpose as a psychoanalyst is "to produce an effect," the movement of the patient from a passive state to an active state in his treatment (*MMSS*, 69).

In this description of psychoanalysis, it is striking that the meaning of reality and the meaning of human action are shifted while the self is made central. It is the reality of the psychic event, not the reality of the engagement with the world that matters. Reality has become "subjective." Action becomes internal, acting upon oneself, not directing one's action to another human being. In the attainment of self-consciousness the modern individual becomes thoroughly self-centered, caught in the closed circle of the objective observer-passive subject.

When Jung describes the fundamental attitude of the psychoanalyst toward his patient, the attitude that the patient himself seeks to attain, he refers to the patient as both a human being and as a subhuman bound to his body like an animal. Man is no longer the animal with reason, the "rational animal" as the tradition would have it. His humanity is identified with consciousness (he is truly a *human* being because of consciousness) while his embodiment is identified with the "subhuman" animal. Embodiment means being "bound" to the animal body. The animal body is no longer an integral part of his humanity for the bond with his body is subhuman.

Jung finds religion to be essential for the modern individual. Man, he says, has always spontaneously developed "religious forms of expression" of religious feelings and ideas (*MMSS*, 122). So there is a strong case for the need for a "religious outlook on life" (*MMSS*, 229). However, Jung does not value religion for its own sake. Religious thoughts, feelings, impulses, attitudes, expressions, and experiences are simply *psychic* realities. Therefore, they must be taken as given, just as dreams are taken, as material for consciousness. "I attribute a positive value to all religions. In their symbolism I recognize those figures which I have met with in the dreams and fantasies of my patients" (*MMSS*, 119).

For Jung, the beliefs and practices of the Christian religion are not responses to the reality of revealed mysteries. Rather they are symbols which cannot be understood literally. "The standpoint of the creeds is archaic; they are full of impressive mythological symbolism which, if taken literally, comes into insufferable conflict with knowledge." But if the statement "Christ rose from the dead" is taken not literally but symbolically, then it can be interpreted so as not to conflict with knowledge (*US*, 37). Jung asks: "Is it not time that the Christian mythology, instead of being wiped out, was understood symbolically for once?" (*US*, 38)

To reduce the history of salvation to mythology and to reduce mystery to symbolism is to deny the historical embodied reality of the incarnation and to spiritualize the incarnation by abstracting a purely human meaning from the incarnation. Jung argues that the Christian mythology should not be wiped out because, so long as it is treated symbolically and not literally, it is the only thing that can transform the human being in the way which psychoanalysis makes possible. "We moderns are faced with the necessity of rediscovering the life of the spirit; we must experience it anew for ourselves. It is the only way we can break the spell that binds us to the cycle of biological events" (*MMSS*, 122). Thus, the spiritual is separated from the biological.

Religious psychic realities free us from nature, as we see in Jung's symbolic interpretation of baptism: "What the Christian sacrament of baptism purports to do is of the greatest importance for the psychic development of mankind. Baptism endows the human being with a unique soul. I do not mean, of course, the baptismal rite in itself as a *magical act* that is effective at one performance. I mean that the *idea* of baptism lifts a man out of his archaic identification with the world and changes him into a being who stands above it. The fact that mankind has risen to the level of this idea is baptism in the deepest sense, for it means the birth of spiritual man who transcends nature" by his own efforts (*MMSS*, 145, emphasis added). The "life of the spirit," then, is the self-conscious life of psychological maturity.

Freedom from nature is, for Jung, the achievement of individuality, a kind of freedom of the individual from the common nature of the animal species. One of the essential symbolic teachings of the Christian religion is the sacrifice of the merely natural man, of the unconscious being who ate the apple in Paradise, for the sake of becoming the "spiritual" man (*MMSS*, 96). The meaning of "the imitation of Christ" is that "we are to live our own proper lives as truly as he lived his" (*MMSS*, 236). At its core, Christianity conveys "a symbol which has for its content the individual way of life of a man, the Son of Man" (*US*, 49).

Repeatedly, Jung insists on the importance of the transcendence of nature and the biological dimension of human life. "Spiritual man ... transcends nature" (*MMSS*, 145). He insists that we must "break the spell that binds us to the cycle of biological events" (*MMSS*, 122). The merely natural man must be sacrificed so that the new man can come into being. "Nature" is our bond with the subhuman animal body. Self-consciousness, however, is "spiritual." The posture of the objective observer in psychoanalysis is for the sake of freedom from nature, freedom from the psychic realities which hold him in the power of nature. In taking the stance of scientific objectivity, he becomes increasingly disembodied and "spiritual." This new meaning of *spirituality* captures the fact that Jung has abstracted a meaning, an idea, from Christianity and uses it in the service of man's self-redemption.

In this act of Gnostic spiritualization, something essential to human being is lost or suppressed. Something is missing from Hulga's personality. Her disembodied and detached mind requires the absence or suppression of what O'Connor refers to as "felt-knowledge" or "blood" knowledge. This suppression is Hulga's heart condition.

Discussing her fiction with Cecil Dawkins, O'Connor writes: "Don't mix up thought-knowledge with felt-knowledge" (*HB*, 491). In her stories, felt-knowledge often takes the form of blood. Blood and the quality of the bloodline are inherited and thus tied to the biological level of human life. Enoch Emery has "wise blood" from his daddy. Throughout *Wise Blood*, he is led by instinct: he "just knows" what to do. Hazel Motes has "wise blood" from his grandfather. In *The Violent Bear It Away*, even Rayber, the psychologist, has "good blood" from Old Tarwater and therefore the possibility of salvation is open to him. In "A Good Man is Hard to Find," the Grandmother tells The Misfit: "I know you're a good man. You don't look a bit like you have common blood. I know you must come from nice people!"[13]

O'Connor's 'blood' can be understood in its similarity to Pascal's 'heart'. Both are responses to the detachment and disembodiment of the

---

13 Montgomery, *Innerleckchuls*, 89, identifies O'Connor's felt-knowledge with the Thomistic *intellectus*. Modern Gnosticism is the condition in which the poles of thought and feeling, *ratio* and *intellectus*, are in conflict with each other in the modern mind. "The scholastic distinguished two modes in the action of man's thought, the *ratio* and the *intellectus*." This distinction, he says, is fundamental to O'Connor although she does not use those technical terms: she refers to the *ratio* as 'thought-knowledge' and the *intellectus* as 'felt-knowledge.' As "an orthodox Christian who practices fiction as an 'incarnational' art, [she] is concerned with both the 'blood' and the 'head' as necessary to her incarnational practice" (68–69). Montgomery identifies the *intellectus* or "felt-knowledge" as the "heart" (73, 85). There are good reasons to associate Thomistic intellect and Pascalian heart. But since Pascal chooses not to use the Thomistic term, we might conclude that his understanding of the heart is his response to modern disembodied mind from his own uniquely modern perspective.

modern mind and to modern philosophy's understanding of the human being as objective observer-passive subject. For the heart is suppressed in the act of philosophical reflection through which the objective observer-passive subject comes into being.

Romano Guardini claims that the heart "is in a certain sense the central reality of Pascal's image of man."[14] In contrast to the disembodied, detached mind of modern philosophy and modern science which rises above nature in order to master nature, Pascal's notion of the heart gives us a picture of an embodied kind of knowing and judging which is integral to human nature. His "discovery" of the heart is his recovery of the pre-reflective, pre-self-conscious dimension of thought and thus his recovery of the human itself from the objective observer-passive subject of modern philosophy.

We can see something of what Pascal means by the heart in the example of the debate over the morality of abortion. Opponents of abortion have long understood that changing attitudes toward abortion is first and foremost a matter of changing hearts, not minds, because the mind follows the heart. The debate over abortion shows us that the heart is not an infallible guide to what is good, for the heart can go terribly wrong: it is possible to be "heartless" and hard-hearted. Both sides of the abortion debate have their arguments. For those opposed to abortion, the argument rests on the humanity of the child in the womb. For proponents, the argument rests on the right of autonomy of the woman. All of the arguments for and against abortion have been set out for decades, yet the conflict remains, for the fundamental difference goes much deeper than reasons and arguments.

Why do some people find the humanity of the child more compelling than the autonomy of the woman? Why do proponents of abortion insist on the scientific objectivity of the term *fetus* to refer to the baby in the womb? Is this difference based on mere feelings and emotions? True,

---

14   Guardini, *Pascal*, 128.

feelings and emotions, as well as the lack of feeling and emotions, do play a role. But more fundamentally, behind or beneath the differences of argument and emotion stands a far more comprehensive orientation of the whole human being to the meaning of human existence, an entire complex of more or less conscious instincts, intuitions, and desires, determining which arguments will move us and which will not.

Both opponents and proponents know the arguments for and against abortion. However, they evaluate them differently. They give priority to either the claim of the baby to humanity or the claim of the mother to autonomy. And this activity of ranking is not based on reason. Reasons can be given but they cannot prove the validity of the most fundamental evaluations. This evaluative activity is a moral judgment, and that is the domain of the heart.

The rightly-ordered human heart is formed in the tradition. For the tradition is not just another "ideology." It is not merely a coherent system of "ideas," a "theory," although it can be examined, studied, and understood. Rather, the tradition includes feelings, intuitions, sensibilities, and practices. This is to say that sacred tradition forms the entire human being, not simply his mind, but more importantly, his heart.

In O'Connor's blood and in Pascal's heart we find what is missing from the truly modern man: a kind of knowledge which depends upon the union of body and mind, and an openness of the human being to the mystery of his incompleteness and of something greater than himself which alone can satisfy his desire for wholeness.

We can identify three activities of the heart as Pascal understands it, that is, as an intuitive and evaluative apprehension of reality. First, the activity of the heart is a kind of knowing. It is of the greatest importance that we avoid attributing any sentimental meaning to the heart. When Guardini asks "What is the heart?" he answers: "One thing above all: It is not the expression of the emotional in opposition to the logical, not feeling in opposition to the intellect, not 'soul' in opposition to 'mind.'

'*Coeur*' is itself mind: a manifestation of the mind. The act of the heart is an act productive of knowledge."[15] As a cognitive faculty, the heart is more fundamental than discursive reasoning. Pascal writes: "We know the truth not only through our reason but also through our heart. It is through the latter that we know first principles, and reason, which has nothing to do with it, tries in vain to refute them" (P, #110).

Second, the activity of the heart is a form of *intuitive* knowledge. For Pascal, certitude rests not on reason but "originates in a totally different sphere—the heart, instinct, and natural insight, these are the names Pascal gives to the intuitive faculty, in his opinion the only one capable of affirming or propounding anything, since reason is limited to working on the data it furnishes."[16] Pascal writes that the principles of intuition "can hardly be

---

15   Guardini, 129.
16   Paul Benichou, *Man and Ethics: Studies in French Classicism*, trans. Elizabeth Hughes (New York: Doubleday, 1971), 92–93. Although Pascal's notion of the heart is central to his understanding of human being, it is one of the most difficult aspects of his philosophy for his interpreters, especially on account of the incomplete and fragmentary character of the *Pensées*. However, scholars do agree on these three activities of the heart. See Nicholas Hammond, "Pascal's *Pensées* and the Art of Persuasion," in *Cambridge Companion to Pascal*, ed. Nicholas Hammond (Cambridge: Cambridge University Press, 2003), 247. "Pascal gives priority to the role of the heart ('*coeur*'), which has nothing to do with sentimental feelings but rather is closely tied to intuition." Pierre Force explains in "Pascal and Philosophical Method," in *Cambridge Companion to Pascal*, ed. Nicholas Hammond (Cambridge: Cambridge University Press, 2003), 220: "In Pascal's psychology the organ that allows us to experience feelings and emotions is the same organ that makes the knowledge of first principles possible. There are thus two paths towards knowing truth: one is rational knowledge, which is discursive and is located in the mind; the other is through the heart; it is intuitive and immediate." Benichou argues, in *Man and Ethics*, 93: "The whole originality of Pascal consists precisely in destroying neither reason nor instinct, in making use of one against the other without building on either, and ultimately, for want of a better solution, assigning all value to instinct, while waiting for grace to touch it."

seen, they are perceived instinctively rather than seen." In intuition, "the thing must be seen all at once, at a glance, and not as a result of progressive reasoning, at least up to a point." In intuition, the mind proceeds "tacitly." Intuitive minds are accustomed "to judge at a glance" (*P*, #512) and judgment is the work of the heart (*P*, #382) "for judgment is what goes with instinct, just as knowledge goes with mind. Intuition falls to the lot of judgment, mathematics to that of mind" (*P*, #513). O'Connor's "blood" refers to this intuitive and instinctive grasp of reality: "O'Connor was aware from reading the work of depth psychologists such as Carl Jung ... that the notion of blood knowledge also refers more generally to the natural intuitive, unconscious knowledge embedded in the human psyche, as distinct from conscious knowledge or supernatural revelation."[17]

Third, "the heart itself is 'mind', but it is *evaluating mind*."[18] The heart is "not some kind of irrational feeling but a spiritual value-experience which founds knowledge in the most precise sense of the word, so much so that there is a logic of the heart, of motives, of value-efficacities." The heart is "the unity of the acts which values experience."[19] Experience, then, is not value-free: judgment is always moral judgment. As Guardini concludes: "Finally, and in a definitive way, the heart is the organ for grasping that value which only manifests itself from above, from revelation: that of the holiness of God, which brings man his fulfillment and his salvation."[20] The heart "perceives" for "it is the heart which perceives God and not the reason. That is what faith is: God perceived by the heart, not by the reason" (*P*, #424).

---

[17] John F. Desmond, "The Lost Childhood of George Rayber," in *Dark Faith: New Essays on Flannery O'Connor's* The Violent Bear It Away, ed. Susan Srigley (Notre Dame, IN: University of Notre Dame Press, 2012), 37.

[18] Romano Guardini, *The Conversion of Augustine*, trans. Elinor Briefs (Providence, RI: Cluny, 2020), 50.

[19] Guardini, *Pascal*, 27.

[20] Guardini, 130–31.

O'Connor points to the heart's openness to mystery, referring to a passage in Romano Guardini's work, *The Lord*. "Msgr. Romano Guardini has written that the roots of the eye are in the heart ... for the Catholic they stretch far and away into the depths of mystery" (*MM*, 144–45). Guardini is commenting on the beatitude, "Blessed are the clean of heart, for they will see God." He explains that "purity of heart means ... a general inner clarity and sincerity of intent before God. Those who possess it see God, for he is recognized not by the bare intellect, but by the inner vision. The eye is clear when the heart is clear, for the roots of the eye are in the heart. To perceive God then, we must purify the heart; it helps little to tax the intellect."[21] To perceive God, Pascal says, is "to see with the eyes of faith" (*P*, #317).

Pascal wants to arouse the desire for truth in the heart for it is the heart which seeks God, motivating the search for truth. "God wishes to move the will rather than the mind. Perfect clarity would help the mind and harm the will" (*P*, #234). And in *The Art of Persuasion*, he speaks of a knowledge that is motivated by love: "when speaking of divine things, [the saints] say that we should love them in order to know them, and that we enter into truth only through love" (*SW*, 203). Pascal, then, finds the proper ordering of the heart in Christian charity: "The heart has its order, the mind has its own, which uses principles and demonstrations. The heart has a different one.... Jesus Christ and St. Paul possess the order of charity, not of the mind, for they wished to humble, not to teach. The same with St. Augustine" (*P*, #298).

Pascal's "discovery" of the heart, then, is his recovery of the human as both essentially embodied and as open and receptive to the givenness of truth. Guardini refers to the heart as "the intermedial realm" where mind and instinct are united, where "mind may become 'flesh and blood',"

---

21 Romano Guardini, *The Lord*, trans. Elinor Castendyk Briefs (Washington, DC: Regnery Publishing, 1996), 81.

and thus experience contact with reality.[22] John McCarthy explains that "at the center of Pascal's investigation of the human things is ... his teaching on the 'heart.' ... the heart constitutes Pascal's real alternative to [modern scientific] method."[23] For "the heart's prompting can only be taken seriously if the human soul is, for all its divisions, disclosive of the wholeness of the whole. In effect, Pascal offers the 'heart' as refutation of the [modern scientific] separation of mind and nature."[24] The heart is Pascal's refutation of the modern philosophical identification of truth with "objectivity." For Pascal, the heart is the embodied cognitive faculty which opens us to faith, to charity, and to holiness, for it points to "our essential dependence upon something 'outside' of us to complete us."[25]

Hulga has "a heart condition." She sees through everything to nothingness, emptiness, and meaninglessness because she cannot escape the closed circle of her own self-consciousness to recognize what is good in itself. When the Bible salesman tells her: "You ain't so smart. I been believing in nothing ever since I was born" (*CS*, 291), he holds up a mirror to her. O'Connor leaves us with the possibility that Hulga, through her humiliating encounter with him, has gained some insight into her own inner hollowness.

---

[22] Guardini, *Conversion of Augustine*, 35–36.
[23] John McCarthy, "Pascal on Certainty and Utility," in *Modern Enlightenment and the Rule of Reason*, ed. John C. McCarthy (Washington, DC: The Catholic University of America Press, 1998), 118.
[24] McCarthy, "Pascal on Certainty and Utility," 97.
[25] McCarthy, 109.

3. Rayber's Solitary Consciousness

*J*ung claims that modern man is solitary "of necessity and at all times" (*MMSS*, 197), for he has broken with the tradition that binds him to his fellow man. He "casts history aside. He wants to break with tradition so that he can experiment with his life and determine what value and meaning things have in themselves, apart from traditional presuppositions" (*MMSS*, 238). Such an individual is "completely modern only when he has come to the very edge of the world, leaving behind him all that has been discarded and outgrown, and acknowledging that he stands before a void out of which all things may grow" (*MMSS*, 197). He has broken free from the tradition and thus isolates himself from participation in the common bond of his culture, for he is self-creating and self-sufficient.

The intended effect of the spiritualization of the incarnation is to make the human being complete in himself, a completeness of man simply as man, without any need for transcendence of the human in union with the divine. The rejection, or suppression, of the need for transcendence of the human and directedness to the divine manifests itself in two closely related characteristics of the truly modern man. First, the modern man makes himself what he wants to be, not guided by any standard outside himself. He is self-contained and self-sufficient with respect to his ethical being. He "saves" himself. Second, the longing for eternal life is suppressed for he must be content with his temporal existence. Indeed, he prides himself on his courage in accepting his mortality and he celebrates his finitude and mutability.

Patrick Ireland describes this "inner" transcendence and self-sufficiency in the terms of modern Gnosticism: "Seeking to discover and liberate within himself that small portion of divinity or Spirit imprisoned by the limitations of his body, the Gnostic must necessarily turn inwardly. Gnostic salvation is thus indistinguishable from narcissistic self-absorption and requires the rejection of the world, especially of the body. The Gnostic's redemptive goal, then, is a sacred self-transcendent unity, like the Godhead's."[1] The transcendent, then, is internalized.

Jung's portrait of the self-creating, self-conscious, self-contained, and self-sufficient modern man emerges in early modern philosophy, in the *Essays* of Montaigne. According to the tradition which Montaigne rejects, the human good is understood in relation to the divine for the human is fulfilled, completed, and perfected only in union with the divine. For Montaigne, however, the desire to rise above the human is the source of the greatest evils. Those who strive for transcendence "want to get out of themselves and escape from the man. That is madness: instead of changing into angels, they change into beasts; instead of raising themselves, they lower themselves. These transcendental humors frighten me" (*E*, 856). In Montaigne's presentation of modern consciousness, Christianity is subjected to the mind of the philosopher and put to use in the modern project of freeing man from his dependence on his all-powerful Creator, thus directing man to himself.

---

1 Patrick J. Ireland, "The Sacred and the Profane: Redefining Flannery O'Connor's Vision," in *Realist of Distances: Flannery O'Connor Revisited*, ed. Karl-Heinz Westarp and Jan Nordby Gretlund (Aarhus: Aarhus University Press, 1987), 189.

Self-consciousness is the reflexive action in which the mind turns back on itself, making itself the center of its action. Montaigne says that "my professed principle ... is to be wholly contained and established within myself" (*E*, 618). He is his own beginning and end, his own center. In this way, self-consciousness is a kind of self-possession: "the greatest thing in the world is to know how to belong to oneself" (*E*, 178).

Montaigne, then, orders his actions not to God or to other human beings but to himself: he is the beginning and the end of his actions. All of his actions are reflexive: "The range of our desires should be circumscribed and restrained to a narrow limit of the nearest and most contiguous good things; and moreover their course should be directed not in a straight line that ends up elsewhere, but in a circle whose two extremities by a short sweep meet and terminate in ourselves. Actions that are performed without this reflexive movement, I mean a searching and genuine reflexive movement ... are erroneous and diseased" (*E*, 773).

The re-ordering of man to himself means that value now comes from man himself, reversing the traditional order in which "the good in itself and for its own sake" is given by nature and divine revelation. When he speaks about "worth," Montaigne moves between the language of "the good," even "the good for its own sake," and the language of "value," thus conflating these two very different meanings.[2] Values are relative to the human will; the good "in itself" is not. Montaigne's project is the re-valuation of all things in relation to the human will. Modern consciousness is the awareness of this power of conferring value. When Jung writes that modern man determines what value and meaning things have "in themselves," he gives expression to the radical reversal in the relation of man to what is good.

Remi Brague explains the idea of value in relation to the modern notion of subjectivity: "The idea of value implies the entrance of the good

---

2   For examples of the way Montaigne conflates worth and value, see *E*, 342; 480–81; 728.

into the orbit of subjectivity.... An important step toward the entrance of the idea of value into the orbit of subjectivity is already found in Montaigne." The shift to the idea of value means that "the good no longer is directly worthwhile, as good, but rather as what has value. It no longer derives its goodness from itself, but from the value assigned to it.... *It is the subject and his power of valorization which then becomes the supreme value.* The subjection of the idea of the good to that of value thus shows itself to be but one more expression of the sovereignty of the modern subject."[3] Man becomes the judge of good and evil, fulfilling his desire for "the knowledge of good and evil" at the source of original sin.

Since man is now directed to himself, not to the divine eternal being of the tradition, modern consciousness must be a consciousness that can be satisfied within itself. Above all, then, the desire for eternal life must be suppressed. Man must not long for the eternal and divine but be content with becoming and changing, within the limits of our temporal existence. As Montaigne says: "I do not portray being: I portray passing" (*E*, 611). Our being is in becoming. The truly modern man embraces his temporality and mutability. He is always on the edge of becoming something new.

Montaigne, then, reduces the meaning of human action to this reflexive movement of the mind. Action is not directed to anything beyond the sovereign self. Indeed, the natural inclinations to union with God and other human beings must be resisted by the self-conscious man. At the very end of the *Essays* Montaigne writes: "It is an absolute perfection and God-like to know how to enjoy *our own being* rightly. We seek other conditions because we do not understand the use of our own, and go outside of ourselves because we do not know what it is like inside" (*E*, 857, emphasis added). Montaigne wants man to be simply merely man. But he means the new modern man, who "knows how" to enjoy his own being "rightly," freed from the power of tradition and directed to himself

---

3   Brague, *Kingdom of Man*, 99–100, emphasis added.

by himself, content with his temporal, mortal life. That is "our own" being, needing nothing outside itself for its fulfillment.

Montaigne's modern man, the self-directed human being who makes himself to be what he wants to be, is the aim of Jung's psychotherapy. Psychoanalysis, when it is truly successful, brings about "a growth of independence, a step toward psychological maturity" (*MMSS*, 70). Psychological maturity leads to "the restoration of the total personality" through the successive assimilation of the unconscious by consciousness. This process is "the bringing into reality of the whole human being," his individuation (*MMSS*, 26). He makes himself an "individual" by breaking free of the constraints of the norms of his culture, becoming self-contained, self-centered, and self-conscious.

Like Montaigne, Jung celebrates the inherent value of becoming. Intense self-consciousness is the experience of being fully in the moment: "He alone is modern who is fully conscious of the present" (*MMSS*, 197). For "only the man who has outgrown the stages of consciousness belonging to the past ... can achieve a full consciousness of the present" (*MMSS*, 197–98). For Jung, the human being is made whole through the transforming power of self-consciousness (*MMSS*, 47). Yet, the wholeness of self-consciousness is not a finished state. The patient "can make himself creatively independent," and "give form to his own inner experience" (*MMSS*, 70). Jung says: "My aim is to bring about a psychic state in which my patient begins to experiment with his own nature—a state of fluidity, change and growth, in which there is no longer anything eternally fixed and hopelessly petrified" (*MMSS*, 66).

Jung describes the general neurosis of our time which most men experience as "the senselessness and emptiness of their lives" (*MMSS*, 61). However, the truly modern man who frees himself from the past and enjoys the most intense self-consciousness finds purpose in his life. He finds that "the center of gravity of the personality" has shifted (*MMSS*, 70). The process of bringing the unconscious to consciousness is a "centering process" in which he attains a "new centre of equilibrium." His feeling of life is heightened and he feels a new sense of purposefulness (*MMSS*, 72). Such an individual instantiates what is best in man: his daring and aspiration (*MMSS*, 239).

Jung claims that a human being who has not yet discovered what life means for him undergoes spiritual suffering. But spiritual suffering gives rise to "creativeness" and psychic progress, for this is the "innermost meaning" of spiritual suffering (*MMSS*, 225). The religious requirement of repentance is not at issue here for "the acceptance of oneself is the essence of the moral problem and the epitome of the whole outlook on life" (*MMSS*, 235). Self-centered and self-satisfied, this new man is closed to the mystery of human existence, indifferent to the great questions that arise within the tradition and, content to live in the moment, indifferent to the possibility of eternal life.

The essential features of modern consciousness, as they are presented in Montaigne and Jung, are displayed with remarkable clarity in the character of Rayber, the psychologist. *The Violent Bear It Away* concerns the members of a family—a dysfunctional family, we might say—and focuses on four members of that family: old Tarwater, young Tarwater, Rayber, and Bishop. O'Connor traces the genealogy of young Tarwater back to his great-uncle, old Tarwater, and old Tarwater's sister, whom old Tarwater describes as a whore. The sister married a man named Rayber and they had two children: a boy (referred to as Rayber throughout the novel) and a girl who is young Tarwater's mother. Rayber, then, is old Tarwater's nephew and young Tarwater's uncle. Rayber's son and young Tarwater's cousin, Bishop, is a "dim-witted" child.

Old Tarwater is a crazy, Christ-obsessed backwoods prophet. His nephew, Rayber, had managed to escape this influence, presumably through the study of psychology, and had become a teacher. Old Tarwater made the terrible mistake of moving in with his nephew Rayber in his time of need. As old Tarwater tells the story to young Tarwater, Rayber had taken him in under the name of charity, but had "at the same time been creeping into his soul by the back door, asking him questions that meant more than one thing, planting traps around the house and watching him fall into them, and finally coming up with a written study of him for a schoolteacher magazine" (*VBA*, 4). Creeping into his soul by the back door, Rayber questioned old Tarwater about his early life. Then he wrote in his published paper: "His fixation of being called by the Lord had its origin in insecurity. He needed the assurance of a call, so he called himself" (*VBA*, 19). The old man's deepest conviction that he had been called by the Lord is merely an illusion, a psychic obsession caused by a psychic need.

For Rayber, the psychologist, his uncle has become merely the subject of his science: old Tarwater is the passive subject of Rayber's objective observation. O'Connor's contrast here between old Tarwater's understanding of charity and Rayber's treatment of his uncle points to the meaning of Rayber's solitary consciousness. The relationship between the objective observer and his passive subject is neither a natural relationship such as the familial bond which Rayber shares with his uncle, nor a supernatural bond of Christian charity. Rayber seems to be incapable of love. As the story develops, it becomes clear that he resists any psychological inclination to love which might break through the closed circle of his own self-consciousness.

When he saw what Rayber was up to, old Tarwater left and returned to his own place in the woods, and set about raising young Tarwater in his own way. Infuriated by Rayber's lies and betrayal, old Tarwater warns young Tarwater never to let Rayber get his hands on him. But when the old man dies, young Tarwater makes his way to Rayber's door and Rayber seizes his second chance at transforming an ignorant, stubborn, backwoods Tarwater into a modern man.

Rayber looks at young Tarwater as a "fascinating problem." He thinks that young Tarwater needs "a monumental job of reconstruction" (*VBA*, 97), and that he, Rayber, is just the man to undertake this. When he begins to see "a solution" to the problem of young Tarwater (*VBA*, 90), he comes up with a "way he could ferret to the center of the emotional infection" (*VBA*, 111), and designs an "experiment" to cure him (*VBA*, 15). Rayber wants to re-create young Tarwater. He wants to make him a new, modern man. The way he actually *is*, the way he was actually created, is not good enough for Rayber, for young Tarwater is not yet fully human.

In his approach to the problem of young Tarwater, Rayber's experiments and manipulations are designed to get Tarwater to see the unconscious motives and irrational impulses that Rayber is bringing to light. "There's a part of your mind that works all the time, that you're not aware of yourself. Things go on in it. All sorts of things you don't know about" (*VBA*, 17). He explains: "You don't even know what makes you do the things you do" (*VBA*, 192). But young Tarwater, like his great-uncle, will have none of it. In his response to Rayber, he shows his understanding of what the psychologist means by the unconscious: "I ain't worried about what my underhead is doing" (*VBA*, 171).

Rayber is trying to save young Tarwater from being a freak like his great-uncle. "You're going to grow up to be a freak if you don't let yourself be helped. You still believe all that crap he taught you. You're eaten up with false guilt" (*VBA*, 173–74). For Rayber, then, the tradition is simply "all that crap." Rayber is determined to save him from his inherited instincts, but the young boy turns out to be consumed by the "family affliction," especially in his inherited obsession with baptizing Rayber's son Bishop. Old Tarwater had baptized Rayber against the wishes of his parents, and young Tarwater will baptize Bishop against the wishes of Rayber.

Rayber sees young Tarwater's urge to baptize Bishop as "a kind of *sickness*" (*VBA*, 151, emphasis in original) and he tells him: "Until you get rid of this compulsion to baptize Bishop, you'll never make any progress toward becoming a normal person. I told you ... that you were going to be a freak.... I want you to make the choice and not simply be driven by a compulsion you don't understand. What we understand, we can control"

(*VBA*, 194). Rayber is attempting to show young Tarwater the value of bringing his unconscious compulsions under the control of consciousness so that he will not be simply determined by what he has inherited but be able to choose what he becomes.[4] However, for O'Connor, Tarwater's compulsion to be a prophet is not a compulsion in the clinical sense, for in his compulsion is "the mystery of God's will for him" (*MM*, 116).

When O'Connor speaks as the narrator in the novel, she gives us further insight into Rayber's psychoanalytic mind. "He gazed through the actual insignificant boy before him to an image of him that he held fully developed in his mind" (*VBA*, 90). In the process of his major reconstruction of young Tarwater, Rayber retained only those aspects of his thoughts about Tarwater that could be "abstracted, clean, into the future person he envisioned" (*VBA*, 179). For Rayber, the real Tarwater is an "idea." The actual Tarwater who stands before him in flesh and blood with his inherited compulsions and struggles is insignificant, to be put aside and forgotten as something unworthy of being a human person. Christina Bieber Lake explains: "When Rayber sees living things with his eyes, he extinguishes the life in them; by straining the mysterious through his brain, he flattens it into a quantifiable chart, book, or set of figures. Thus Rayber treats the inexplicable in the same fashion as does the modern scientist.... The end result is the elimination—to Rayber's mind anyway—of mystery."[5] Rayber's "idea" of Tarwater is the limit

---

4   The process of bringing the unconscious impulses and inclinations to consciousness, is displayed throughout Montaigne's *Essays*, especially in "Of the resemblance of children to fathers." Given the great emphasis which psychoanalysis places on the role of parents in the formation of their children's unconscious impulses, the title of this essay is especially apt. Montaigne writes that "all those predispositions that are born in us without reason are bad; they are a kind of disease that we must combat" (*E*, 580). Inherited inclinations are merely "stupid and thoughtless" (*E*, 597). He describes the way he approaches the inherited predispositions that he finds in himself, submitting them to the power of his own judgment.

5   Lake, *Incarnational Art*, 151.

of the reality of Tarwater, the only way he sees him as he pushes him toward what he wants him to be.

Rayber explains his understanding of human dignity to young Tarwater, hoping to free the boy from his bondage to his past and show him what it really means to be a man. This understanding is expressed in terms of the spiritualization of the sacrament of baptism and the meaning of redemption: "The great dignity of man is his ability to say: I am born once and no more. What I can see and do for myself and my fellowman in this life is all of my portion and I'm content with it. *It's enough to be a man.*" He explains to young Tarwater why he refuses to baptize Bishop: "I have the guts to maintain my self-respect and not to perform futile rites over him. I have the guts not to become the prey of superstitions. He is what he is and there's nothing for him to be born into. *My guts are in my head*" (VBA, 172, emphasis added). There is here an essential connection between Rayber's claims that "it is enough to be a man" and that his guts are in his head, for he shows what he means by 'man,' identifying his humanness with his mind. To say that his guts are in his head is to reject the reality of his "heart," a rejection which is the denial of his capacity for love.

For Rayber, young Tarwater's inherited compulsion to baptize Bishop is nothing more than a meaningless unconscious drive. "Baptism is only an empty act. If there's any way to be born again, it's a way that you accomplish yourself, an understanding about yourself that you reach after a long time, perhaps a long effort" (VBA, 194). Rayber explains: "It's the way I've chosen for myself. It's the way you take as a result of being born again the natural way—through your own efforts. Your intelligence" (VBA, 195). In the real world, "there's no saviour but yourself" (VBA, 76). Rayber is indifferent even to his own dissolution, for he believed that "this indifference was the most that human dignity could achieve" (VBA, 200). He prides himself on his courage in accepting his own mortality.

Yet, beneath the carefully maintained surface of objectivity, rationality, and self-containment, Rayber is really deeply troubled and divided within himself, a division that displays itself especially in his relation with his own son. Rayber is "a modern Manichean." He is "abstracted—drawn up into thought—as much as he is disengaged from the life of the flesh. He wishes to live in the realm of pure thought."[6] But O'Connor, as narrator, tells us that Rayber "kept himself upright on a very narrow line between madness and emptiness" (*VBA*, 115). It seems that he tries to embrace and be content with the emptiness of his life while he is terrified of losing his mind. He wants to be all mind, to control everything by understanding everything, but the reality of his embodiment forces him to see how easily he can lose his grip on his mind. He is forced up against the limits of self-consciousness and is pushed to face himself.

Rayber "saw himself divided in two—a violent and a rational self" (*VBA*, 139). His rational self wants to contain him, to control the irrational desires and impulses, bringing them under the power of consciousness. Pity and rage seem to be the only emotions that Rayber allows himself to experience. When he encounters young Tarwater's stupid resistance to his reconstruction, his feelings "alternated drastically between compassion for [Tarwater's] haunted look and fury at the way he was treated by him" (*VBA*, 152). Rayber explains to young Tarwater that his great uncle is "only worth our pity." And he warns him: "You want to avoid extremes. They are for violent people" (*VBA*, 145).

The object of Rayber's pity is Tarwater's bondage to the past, to the irrational superstitions and inherited obsessions born of the futile desire for eternal life. Rayber's pity "encompassed all exploited children" (*VBA*, 131). So, when he looks at young Tarwater, he sees an exploited child who has the potential for freedom and self-consciousness. Rayber wants him to develop into "a useful man" (*VBA*, 92). But when he looks at his own

---

6   Jason Peters, "Abstraction and Intimacy in Flannery O'Connor's *The Violent Bear It Away*," in *Dark Faith: New Essays on Flannery O'Connor's The Violent Bear It Away*, ed. Susan Srigley (Notre Dame, IN: University of Notre Dame Press, 2012), 91.

son, Bishop, he says: "Five years old for all eternity, useless forever" (*VBA*, 34). Rayber, then, sees human beings as either useful or useless. Human dignity is for him seen only in terms of usefulness. When Rayber sees young Tarwater's fixation on Bishop, he tells him: "Just forget Bishop exists.... He's just a mistake of nature" (*VBA*, 117). Bishop's existence is meaningless because he is useless. O'Connor is showing us that, without the relationship to the divine, the human being is reduced to an object of use. Rayber cannot see the contradiction in his own position. He pities all exploited children, but he himself values children in terms of their usefulness. The existence of Bishop stands as the great contradiction to his reduction of worth to usefulness.

Rayber sees Bishop as a "problem," but when old Tarwater saw Bishop for the first time, "he beheld an unspeakable mystery" (*VBA*, 32). Rayber's insoluble problem is Tarwater's wondrous mystery. Indeed, old Tarwater sees himself in the little boy: "Bishop looked like the old man grown backwards to the lowest form of innocence" (*VBA*, 111). Bishop stands there "dim and ancient, like a child who had been a child for centuries" (*VBA*, 91). O'Connor has taken us to the lowest level of conscious life, to a child who lives at the edge of consciousness, to an ancient memory of innocence. As old Tarwater tells us: "the Lord gave [Rayber] one he couldn't corrupt" (*VBA*, 77).

Rayber sees Bishop as an insoluble problem because Bishop forces him to confront something within himself. The sub-rational boy brings him face-to-face with his own irrational feelings. Rayber divides the human into rational and irrational. He "had not conquered the problem of Bishop. He had only learned to live with it and had learned too that he could not live without it" (*VBA*, 112). Rayber's inability to live without the mystery of Bishop points to the possibility of integrity for him, but he can only see it as a curse. There were moments when "rushing from some inexplicable part of himself, he would experience a love for the child so outrageous that he would be left shocked and depressed for days, and trembling for his sanity. It was only a touch of the curse that lay in his blood" (*VBA*, 112–13). Rayber attributes this irrational and therefore inexplicable reaction to a psychic disposition inherited from old Tarwater, an unconscious impulse which he has not yet succeeded in bringing under the control of his consciousness. Sometimes "he would feel himself overwhelmed by the horrifying love.... If, *without thinking*, he lent himself to it, he would feel suddenly a morbid surge of the love that terrified him—powerful enough to throw him to the ground in an act of idiot praise. It was completely irrational and abnormal" (*VBA*, 113, emphasis added). The idiocy of Bishop is there in him. In the experience of his love for Bishop, he is brought to the edge of worship, where his entire self-satisfied life is revealed in its emptiness.

Commenting on Rayber's love for Bishop, O'Connor writes: "I think the strongest of Rayber's psychological pulls are in the direction that he does not ultimately choose" (*HB*, 488). Rayber has to regard the psychological pull of his love for Bishop as irrational, as a merely sub-human impulse arising out of his unconscious. He suppresses his humanity, resisting the promptings of his heart to risk everything and lose himself in his love for his son.

As a psychologist, Rayber knew the value of love and how it could be used to transform people: he understood the usefulness of love. But "none of this had the least bearing on his situation. The love that would overcome him was of a different order entirely. It was not the kind that could be used for the child's improvement or his own. It was love without reason, love for something futureless, *love that appeared to exist only to be itself*, imperious and all demanding, the kind that would cause him to make a fool of himself in an instant" (*VBA*, 113–14, emphasis added). A love that exists only to be itself would have to be irrational for Rayber. In his love for Bishop, which he does not choose, Rayber has the chance to transcend the limits of the rational and the useful.

Rayber knew that "his own stability depended on the little boy's presence. He could control his terrifying love as long as it had its focus in Bishop, but if anything happened to the child, he would have to face it in itself" (*VBA*, 182). The presence of Bishop allows him to keep himself together, as it were. It is young Tarwater who, in his own way, sees the truth about Rayber. When Rayber picks up Bishop and holds him tight, young Tarwater "had a vision of the schoolteacher and his child as inseparably joined.... The child might have been a deformed part of [Rayber] that had been accidentally revealed" (*VBA*, 93). Bishop reveals the terrible division within Rayber himself.

It is Rayber's love for Bishop that holds out the possibility of Rayber's redemption. After all, Rayber is the nephew of old Tarwater, and as old Tarwater tells us about his nephew: "Good blood flows in his veins" (*VBA*, 59). And old Tarwater is convinced that, in spite of Rayber's apparent contempt for him, "he loved me like a daddy and he was ashamed of it" (*VBA*, 71). Somehow, Rayber knew that old Tarwater, the prophet who had baptized him against the wishes of his parents, was the only one who really loved him.

In one of the most remarkable exchanges in this novel, old Tarwater explains the way in which Bishop confronts Rayber with the limits of his own self-consciousness: "He wanted it all in his head. You can't change a child's pants in your head" (*VBA*, 75). Rayber expected a child he could mold and form into a psychologically mature and useful man. Instead he is given a child who cannot be molded (or as old Tarwater says, corrupted) and whose pants have to be changed.

On the one hand, Rayber thinks that Bishop is sub-human: Bishop is not capable of self-consciousness. On the other hand, he feels an irrational love for him. There is no connection between these two parts of himself. Or rather, they are in conflict with one another. If he saw Bishop as human, fully human, his love for him would make sense. Christina Bieber Lake explains: "Rayber loves Bishop in spite of himself, and he can make no sense of that love. Accustomed to seeing love only as a tool that can be used to transform psychological 'cases' when nothing else works, Rayber recognizes his own love for Bishop as of another order entirely." Because "there is no *reason* for the child to live," Rayber cannot make sense of his love.[7]

In a letter to Betty Hester, O'Connor writes: "Rayber's love for Bishop is the purest love I have ever dealt with. It is because of its terrifying purity that Rayber has to destroy it" (*HB*, 379). It is pure because it is not useful, but exists only to be itself. "Rayber did love him, but throughout the book he was fighting his inherited tendency to mystical love. He had the idea that his love could be contained in Bishop but if Bishop were gone, there would be nothing to contain it and he would then love everything and specifically Christ" (*HB*, 484–85).

In the character of Rayber, O'Connor shows us the suppression of the human heart in the radical division between spirit and matter within the truly modern man. Through Rayber's internal conflicts, O'Connor shows us both the depths of the deformity of modern consciousness and the possibility of redemption. In the novel as a whole, this possibility of redemption is worked out most fully in the contrasts between Rayber and young Tarwater, and is ultimately set within the context of the Catholic sacramental view of life and the mutual interdependence of human agents.

Old Tarwater says of Rayber: "It was me could act, not him. He could never take action" (*VBA*, 76). Rayber cannot really act because he is the objective observer-passive subject. All of the movements of his mind are reflexive, occurring within the closed circle of his self-conscious mind. For old Tarwater and, eventually, for young Tarwater, action is centered around a baptism. But the meaning of the action is more than the visible immersion in water and the audible sounds of the Trinitarian formula—what Rayber calls a meaningless rite. O'Connor's presentation of the action in its violence and confusion brings out the way in which divine grace shows itself as a possibility. The violence of the baptism reveals the conflict of wills within young Tarwater.

---

[7] Lake, *Incarnational Art*, 155.

In the encounters between Rayber and both old and young Tarwater, two very different visions of human freedom emerge. For Rayber, the psychoanalyst, freedom is freedom from the tradition, from the past, from history, and from nature. Freedom means bringing the unconscious impulses under the control of consciousness, liberating oneself from the instincts that cause conflict within us. Freedom is self-consciousness. Rayber judges the brand of independence the old man had wrought in young Tarwater, not as a constructive independence but rather as irrational, backwoods, and ignorant (*VBA*, 100). Rayber tells old Tarwater that young Tarwater is "going to be his own saviour. He's going to be free!" (*VBA*, 70).

For both Tarwaters, however, freedom remains something mysterious, something that cannot be captured in the psychologist's science. Rayber wants young Tarwater to know "that there was someone who knew exactly what went on inside him and who understood it for the good reason that it was understandable" (*VBA*, 187). But old Tarwater had explained to young Tarwater why he saved him from being brought up by Rayber: "I saved you to be free, your own self! ... and not a piece of information inside his head!" (*VBA*, 16). And young Tarwater echoes this angry declaration when he realizes what Rayber is trying to do to him: "I'm free. I'm outside your head. I ain't in it. I ain't in it and I ain't about to be" (*VBA*, 111).

Young Tarwater is a reluctant prophet. He does not want to be like his old great-uncle. He does not want to baptize Bishop, yet he feels compelled to baptize him. Tarwater had all along avoided Bishop and wanted nothing to do with him, perhaps because he was determined to resist the compulsion to baptize him. Then one day, he suddenly "knew that the child *recognized* him" (*VBA*, 93). Bishop recognized Tarwater as the one who had been sent to baptize him. When Rayber takes them to the lake, the conflict is played out in the interactions of young Tarwater and Bishop. Tarwater sees his chance to drown Bishop, an act of murder that Rayber himself admits he had tried but was unable to do. Now Tarwater, who could not even bring himself to look Bishop in the eye, looks "triumphantly, boldly, in the very center of [Bishop's] eyes" (*VBA*, 177). He says defiantly to Rayber that he can destroy his inherited compulsion: "I can pull it up by the roots, once and for all. I can do something. I ain't like you. All you can do is think what you would have done if you had done it. Not me. I can do it. I can act" (*VBA*, 196).

Bishop's recognition of young Tarwater and Tarwater's determination to act bring the two cousins together. Rayber is startled to see Tarwater put his hand on Bishop's neck and lead him out the door to the boat. As young Tarwater and Bishop go off together, Rayber watches the "two figures, hatted and somehow ancient, bound together by some necessity of nerve that excluded him." Yet, it seemed to Rayber "that it was Bishop who was doing the leading, that the child had made the capture" (*VBA*, 196–97).

O'Connor tells us that Bishop is "a kind of Christ image" or "a kind of redemptive figure" (*HB*, 191). Christina Bieber Lake points to the way in which Bishop is a figure of Christ for O'Connor: "Tarwater must recognize that his calling is of the highest because it is of the lowest. This struggle to see Bishop correctly explains why Bishop operates as a kind of Christ figure. He is the lowliest of the low, and it is shocking that God would value him, as shocking as the fact that God would incarnate himself as a human baby." When Tarwarter bends down to tie Bishop's shoelaces, he humbles himself before the innocent boy.[8]

The last time that we see Rayber is at the moment when he realizes that young Tarwater is drowning Bishop: "The point where Tarwater is drowning Bishop is the point where he [Rayber] has to choose. He makes the Satanic choice, and the inability to feel the pain of his loss is the immediate result. His collapse then may indicate that he is not going to be able to sustain his choice—but that is another book maybe. Rayber

---

8 Lake, *Incarnational Art*, 158.

and Tarwater are really fighting the same current in themselves. Rayber wins out against it and Tarwater loses. Rayber achieves his own will, and Tarwater submits to his vocation." O'Connor, however, leaves open the possibility of Rayer's salvation: "There is too much in there about Rayber's struggling against the seed that is in him to take him entirely for the devil. I would have liked for him to be saved, and it is ambiguous whether he may be or not" (*HB*, 357).

After young Tarwater drowns Bishop, he knew that he had baptized the child even as he had drowned him, "that he was headed for everything the old man had prepared for him," and that he was moving toward "a violent encounter with his fate" (*VBA*, 203). Later, he confesses: "It was an accident. I didn't mean to.... I only meant to drown him. You're only born once. They were just some words that ran out of my mouth and spilled in the water" (*VBA*, 209). When he says "it was an accident" we might have expected him to mean that the drowning was an accident, but he wants to insist that it was the baptism that was an accident. He *acted*, but the action is still confused in his mind. He did what he did not want to do. The drowning is a baptism. The baptism is a death and a second birth.

Finally the conflict within him breaks out in his dream-like memory of the drowning, and "suddenly in a high raw voice the defeated boy cried out the words of baptism, shuddered, and opened his eyes" (*VBA*, 216). As Christian Bieber Lake puts it: Tarwater "feels both the overpowering guilt of having murdered an innocent child and the sacramental significance of the literal acting out of a Christian's being buried with Christ in baptism so that he can be raised again. Tarwater began here to enter that death too, a death to self that he has never before achieved."[9] Tarwater's "defeat" is, at the same time, his free act.

O'Connor brings out the mystery of human freedom through the possibility of grace in this moment where the action might be a drowning, an act

---

9   Lake, *Incarnational Art*, 176.

of murder, or it might be a baptism in which Bishop is reborn. It is either the deliberate killing of a sub-human accident of nature, or the recognition of this child as fully human, his existence freely willed by his creator.

Rayber says that "the great dignity of man is his ability to say: I am born once and no more" (*VBA*, 34). O'Connor, however, is showing us baptism as an act of acknowledging inherent human dignity. In his compulsion to baptize Bishop, Tarwater is, knowingly or unknowingly, acknowledging Bishop as a human being, possessing an inherent and infinite worth.

Young Tarwater becomes a prophet in a way that he could not have foreseen. He had wanted the Lord's call to be a voice from out of a clear and empty sky "untouched by any fleshly hand or breath." He did everything he could to avoid the strange and terrifying "intimacy of creation" (*VBA*, 22). But in fact "the Lord out of dust had created him, had made him blood and nerve and mind, had made him to bleed and weep and think, and set him in a world of loss and fire all to baptize one idiot child *that He need not have created in the first place* and to cry out a gospel just as foolish" (*VBA*, 91–92, emphasis added). Tarwater has come to understand more deeply the meaning of creation.

The Violent Bear It Away expresses O'Connor's sacramental view of life in an especially clear way. The action of baptizing Bishop is the dramatic, violent revelation of young Tarwater's transformation into a prophet like his great-uncle. The change that occurs in him is also presented in terms of the ultimate recognition of his inherited hunger for the bread of life. O'Connor writes that: "The whole action of the novel is Tarwater's selfish will against all that the little lake (the baptismal font) and the bread stand for. This book is a very minor hymn to the Eucharist" (*HB*, 387).

Just as young Tarwater resists the compulsion to baptize, he denies the hunger that he has inherited from the old man. Old Tarwater's hunger was for "the Lord Jesus Himself, the bread of life!" (*VBA*, 62). He spoke constantly of "spending eternity eating the bread of life" (*VBA*, 8). When old Tarwater said that "Jesus is the bread of life," young Tarwater knew that inside him was "the certain, undeniable knowledge that he was not hungry for the bread of life." When the old man said that as soon as he died, he would hasten to the banks of the Lake of Galilee to eat the loaves and the fishes that the Lord had multiplied, "the boy sensed that this was the heart of his great-uncle's madness, this hunger, and what he was secretly afraid of was that it might be passed down, might be hidden in the blood and might strike some day in him and then he would be torn by hunger like the old man, the bottom split out of his stomach so that nothing would heal or fill it but the bread of life" (*VBA*, 21).

When young Tarwater struggles with the drowning-baptism of Bishop, he says defiantly: "I had to prove I wasn't no prophet and I've proved it.... There are them that can act and them that can't, and them that are hungry and them that ain't. That's all. I can act. And I ain't hungry" (*VBA*, 210). He knows that the meaning of his action, confused as it is in his mind, is somehow inseparable from his inherited hunger. His denial that his action was really a baptism is tied to his denial of his inherited hunger: "I ain't hungry for the bread of life" (*VBA*, 211).

Yet the conflict within young Tarwater was always there: in his denials of his inherited burden, there was always the instinctual knowledge that he would become what he did not want to become: "He knew that he was called to be a prophet and that the ways of his prophecy would not be remarkable.... [He watched] his own stricken image of himself, trudging into the distance in the bleeding stinking mad shadow of Jesus, until he at last received his reward, a broken fish, a multiplied loaf" (*VBA*, 91–92).

The novel concludes with young Tarwater, returning to the burnt out place of his home, looking out over the empty field and "feeling a hunger *too great to be contained inside him*" (*VBA*, 237, emphasis added). As he looks, the field appeared to be no longer empty but filled with a multitude of people seated on the hillside, being fed from a basket of bread and fishes. He searches the crowd for his great-uncle and finally sees him lowering himself to the ground, then waiting for the basket to reach him. Young Tarwater recognized at last the object of his hunger, "aware that it was the same as the old man's and that nothing on earth would fill him. His hunger was so great that he could have eaten all the loaves and fishes after they were multiplied" (*VBA*, 241).

The change that occurs in young Tarwater is not a psychological improvement in his level of self-consciousness. On the contrary, it is the outcome of the mysterious struggle of human freedom. Tarwater is changed in ways that he did not intend or want and in ways that he could not have anticipated. The radical shift in the center of his existence from himself to Christ is captured in the image of an inherited hunger that can only be satisfied by the bread of life. In this shifting of the center, Tarwater's heart and mind are finally united in an action that is not self-consciously "reflexive" but truly free because it ends not in himself alone but in his more-than-natural kinship with Bishop. In this sacramental act of mutual interdependence, his solitary modern consciousness is overcome.

4. The Head-Doctor and The Misfit's Guilty Conscience

*B*oth Freud and Jung recognize the phenomenon of the experience of guilt in modern man, but they deny the historical reality of original sin. O'Connor says that Jung understands the "myth" of original sin as nothing more than "Adam's relatively insignificant 'slip-up' with Eve" (*HB*, 382). In "A Good Man Is Hard to Find," the psychological explanation of The Misfit's conduct is expressed in terms of Freud's theory of the Oedipus Complex, rather than in the terms of Jung's psychology. Nevertheless, the main point is the same: both Freud and Jung find the source of this guilt in an "ethical violation" of the norms of a merely traditional morality. From that perspective, the guilt which The Misfit experiences is not grounded in the historical reality of original sin, the fall of man, but is nothing more than a psychic reality to be brought under the therapeutic power of psychoanalysis.

"A Good Man Is Hard to Find" concerns a family—a grandmother, her son, his wife, and two children—who set out on a vacation and encounter three escaped convicts, led by a man who calls himself The Misfit. O'Connor describes this story in terms of the interactions between the Grandmother and

The Misfit. "It is the Grandmother who first recognizes The Misfit and who is most concerned with him throughout. The story is a duel of sorts between the Grandmother and her superficial beliefs and The Misfit's more profoundly felt involvement with Christ's action which set the world off balance for him" (*HB*, 437). Indeed, The Misfit displays a much deeper understanding of the human condition and of the meaning of the Christian mystery than does the superficial Grandmother.

In The Misfit's account of his own life, the mystery of original sin is central. He cannot fully explain why he had been imprisoned for he cannot remember exactly what he did to deserve such punishment. "It was a head-doctor at the penitentiary said what I had done was kill my daddy but I known that for a lie" (*CS*, 130). It appears that the "head-doctor" had diagnosed the cause of The Misfit's criminal deeds in the terms of Freudian psychoanalysis. But The Misfit knows that that is a lie for he has a deeper understanding of his guilt than the psychiatrist has with his theories and abstractions.

The Misfit expresses his sense of the mystery of original sin as a kind of injustice: "I found out the crime don't matter. You can do one thing or you can do another, kill a man or take a tire off his car, because sooner or later you're going to forget what it was you done and just be punished for it.... I call myself The Misfit because I can't make what all I done wrong fit what all I gone through in punishment." When he tries to match his punishment with his crimes, he has the sense that he has not been treated fairly. Why should he be punished for something he can't remember doing? On the other hand, he recognizes the innocence of Christ and the injustice of Christ's punishment: "Jesus thrown everything off balance. It was the same case with Him as with me except He hadn't committed any crime and they could prove I had committed one because they had the papers on me. Of course, they never shown me my papers" (*CS*, 130–31).

In spite of his sense of injustice and helplessness in the face of the psychiatrist's judgment, The Misfit sees that he does have a choice. "Jesus was the only One that ever raised the dead and he shouldn't have done it. He thrown everything off balance. If He did what He said, then it's nothing for you to do but throw everything away and follow him, and if he didn't, then it's nothing for you to do but enjoy the few minutes you got left the best way you can—by killing somebody or burning down his house or doing some other meanness to him. No pleasure but meanness" (CS, 132). The Misfit shows his capacity for understanding the meaning of redemption when he reveals that what it demands is to "throw everything away and follow him."

He sees the choice clearly, but he cannot bring himself to throw everything away and follow Christ because he did not see, with his own eyes, that Christ raised the dead. When the Grandmother says that maybe Jesus did not raise the dead, The Misfit says: "I wasn't there so I can't say he didn't. I wisht I had of been there. It ain't right I wasn't there because if I had of been there I would of known and I wouldn't be like I am now" (CS, 132). Here he reveals his sense of his own sinfulness: "I wouldn't be like I am now." He realizes that he cannot redeem himself, but he cannot make the choice of faith.

As The Misfit confronts his own condition, his voice begins to crack, and the Grandmother, forgetting her own desperate circumstances, suddenly reaches out to him in a moment of unselfishness: "Why you're one of my babies. You're one of my own children!" She touched him on the shoulder and The Misfit "sprang back as if a snake had bitten him" and shot her three times in the chest (CS, 132).

O'Connor describes this scene, this moment in which grace is offered: "The Grandmother is at last alone, facing The Misfit. Her head clears for an instant and she realizes, even in her limited way, that she is responsible for the man before her and joined to him by ties of kinship which have their roots deep in the mystery she has been merely prattling about so far. And at this point, she does the right thing, she makes the right gesture," the gesture which "somehow made contact with mystery" (MM, 111–12).

Once again, The Misfit reveals his capacity for understanding something of the mystery of redemption. As he calmly stands there cleaning his glasses after murdering the Grandmother, he says: "She would of been a good woman if it had been somebody there to shoot her every minute of her life" (*CS*, 133). He recognizes, then, the goodness of her gesture toward him. He recognizes that that is what goodness is. His choice to reject it makes O'Connor's point that "cutting yourself off from Grace is a very decided matter, requiring a real choice, act of will, and affecting the very ground of the soul" (*HB*, 389–90). This moment of grace, O'Connor says "excites the devil to frenzy" (*HB*, 373). Yet, O'Connor does not want to equate The Misfit with the devil. "I prefer to think that, however unlikely this may seem, the old lady's gesture, like the mustard-seed, will grow to be a great crow-filled tree in the Misfit's heart, and will be enough of a pain to him there to turn him into the prophet he was meant to become. But that's another story" (*MM*, 112–13). As with Rayber, the character of The Misfit leaves him open to the possibility of grace.[1]

The Misfit is a prophet-freak. He is a freak because he doesn't "fit," and he is a prophet because he knows that he doesn't fit. He sees his situation in terms of a guilt that he cannot understand. As O'Connor says of all her freaks, they are essentially no more strange than any other human being. They reveal to us our common condition of guilt due to the reality of original sin. O'Connor describes The Misfit as a "spoiled prophet" (*HB*, 465) for he sees clearly the meaning of the incarnation: "He thrown everything off balance." But he cannot bring himself to choose to believe in the reality of the incarnation, that unique intervention in human history which has made the choice to follow Christ or reject him inevitable.

---

1   For a discussion of the possibility of The Misfit's redemption, see Marshall Bruce Gentry, *Flannery O'Connor's Religion of the Grotesque* (Jackson, MS and London: University Press of Mississippi, 1986), 108–12.

The Misfit's insight that Christ "thrown everything off balance" reflects Pascal's fundamental philosophical claim that man does not "fit" within nature, and that this displacement is due to original sin and points to the need for redemption. Pascal concludes that man does not fit within nature because he sees the inadequacies of pre-modern classical-Christian philosophy and science and because he sees the inability of modern philosophy and science to account for human existence.

The world of pre-modern philosophy and science was a finite, integrated whole, a cosmos, ordered to the good, in which each kind of thing had its proper place. Man had his own unique place within that whole, within the hierarchy of nature, between angels and beasts. He "fit" within nature, in spite of his recognition of his fallenness, and could understand himself within that divinely ordered cosmos. The world of pre-modern science was a world of Aristotelian forms and ends which explain why things are the way they are. The divine ordering of the world means that each kind of being is directed by nature to its own perfection. This is a world in which man is at home, for he can gain from nature the wisdom he needs to guide his life.

Modern science makes it impossible for man to continue to understand himself in terms of the pre-modern philosophy of nature and thus makes it impossible for him to gain from nature the wisdom he needs to attain the good: his moral life and his fulfillment can no longer be accounted for in terms of his place within the natural world. The inability of modern science to account for his being, then, actually gives him greater clarity about his true condition. As Thomas Hibbs explains: "Pascal insists that the power and intelligibility of the Christian claim are more evident in the aftermath of modern science than they were in the comfortable premodern cosmos."[2]

---

2   Thomas Hibbs, *Wagering on an Ironic God: Pascal on Faith and Philosophy* (Waco, TX: Baylor University Press, 2017), 192.

Pascal believed that the medieval Scholastic approach to nature was gravely flawed. "His own scientific writings often betray his impatience with the tendency found in the Schools to substitute speculative dicta for careful observation of phenomena."[3] Therefore, he breaks with the Aristotelian tradition of scientific inquiry which persisted through the middle ages. Pascal also criticizes the medieval practice of natural theology. The world of pre-modern philosophy and science lends itself to arguments for the existence of God, the intelligence who designed the world, directing each kind of being to its good. Pascal, however, says that "it is a remarkable fact that no canonical author has ever used nature to prove God.... This is very noteworthy" (P, #463). Metaphysical proofs for the existence of God are "remote and make little impact" (P, #190) for "it is not only impossible but useless to know God without Christ" (P, #191). Pascal, then, abhors the modern philosophical theology of deism which posits a god who sets the world in motion (Descartes's god) but has nothing to do with human life. Deism, he says, is "almost as remote from the Christian religion as atheism" (P, #449).

Pascal does not look to nature for the manifestation of the hidden God: "I shall not undertake here to prove by reasons from nature either the existence of God, or the Trinity or the immortality of the soul, or anything of that kind" not only because such arguments are unconvincing, but "because such knowledge without Christ is useless and sterile" (P, #448). Metaphysical proofs give us Aristotle's First Unmoved Mover, the First Efficient Cause, but not the hidden God of the Bible. As John McCarthy argues: "Pascal expressed hesitations about the properly theological worth of ordinary natural theology: it is impossible thereby to 'see' the biblical God, who reveals to man that he hides himself."[4]

---

3 McCarthy, "Pascal on Certainty and Utility," 98.
4 McCarthy, 123.

Medieval theology defines itself, in the terms of Augustine, Anselm, and Aquinas, as "faith seeking understanding." Theology begins from faith: its first principles are the articles of faith. It then uses philosophy as its handmaiden to better understand what is already believed and held through faith. Pascal, on the other hand, begins from experience, a philosophical beginning, not from faith. In a sense, then, Pascal reverses the medieval formula from "faith seeking understanding" to "understanding seeking faith."[5] As Leszek Kolakowski puts it, for Pascal, "the whole of Christian philosophical, theological, and moral teaching is ultimately about a single question: how is the reality of our worldly experience related to the primordial, creative, infinite divine reality which in the realm of finite things is both manifested and concealed?"[6] Pascal must answer that question against the background of the emergence of the new science which displaces the human being from the natural world.

Pascal, then. breaks with both pre-modern science and medieval natural theology, and he embraces modern science in its experimental approach to nature. However, as Thomas Hibbs describes him, Pascal is "an eccentric modern." Like other modern philosophers, "he repudiates the classical Aristotelian notion of purposiveness in natural nonhuman beings. Much less would he affirm any cosmic teleological harmony. He thinks, writes, and lives in the wake of the shattering of ancient and medieval cosmology. And yet, unlike many of his contemporaries, he retains the notion of a telos of human desire."[7] That is, although Pascal pursues the study of mathematics and natural science in the spirit of the new science,

---

5 Hammond, "Pascal's *Pensées* and the Art of Persuasion," 235: "Far from being a traditional apologia of the Christian religion, [the *Pensées*] not only confronts but also assumes many of the ideas held by those sceptics and non-believers at whom the work is generally thought to be targeted."

6 Leszek Kolakowski, *God Owes Us Nothing: A Brief Remark on Pascal's Religion and on the Spirit of Jansenism* (Chicago: University of Chicago Press, 1995), 182.

7 Hibbs, *Wagering on an Ironic God*, 10.

he does not accept the fundamental orientation of modern philosophy for the study of man himself. While the scientific method of experimentation can give us the truth about non-human nature, it cannot teach us anything about our own being and the meaning of our existence. Pascal writes: "When I began the study of man I saw that these abstract sciences are not proper to man, and that I was straying further from my true condition by going into them than were others by being ignorant of them.... [The] study of man is his true and proper study" (P, #687).

Baron von Hügel sets out two possible approaches to modern science: to see it as self-sufficient or to see it as a part of the whole and as actually pointing to the strangeness of man.[8] Pascal takes the latter approach: modern science cannot account for the meaning of man's existence. In its very failure to offer a foundation for human self-understanding, modern science shows us that man is not at home in the world and thus exposes our essential "displacement." When Paul Griffiths pursues the question of why we should read Pascal, he arrives at the single insight that drives Pascal's inquiry, an insight into the strangeness and incomprehensibility of the human being. The nonhuman cosmos reveals its indifference to man, forcing us to realize our insignificance, so that we become strange to ourselves.[9] Pascal describes the true condition of fallen man, the condition of darkness and anxiety: "Man does not know the place he should occupy. He has obviously gone astray; he has fallen from his true place and cannot find it again. He searches everywhere, anxiously but in vain, in the midst of impenetrable darkness" (P, #400).

Although modern science allows us to see our displacement within nature more clearly, it cannot dispel the darkness and anxiety of our true

---

8   Baron Friedrich von Hügel, *The Mystical Element of Religion as Studied in Saint Catherine of Genoa and Her Friends*, 2nd ed. (New York: E. P. Dutton and Co., 1923), 1:45.

9   Paul J. Griffiths, *Why Read Pascal?* (Washington, DC: The Catholic University of America Press, 2021), 212.

condition. In his study of man, Pascal sees that something essential is suppressed in the transformation of the human being into the objective observer-passive subject of modern science. Pascal cannot take the stance of the objective observer-passive subject in the study of man because he recognizes the central place of the heart in human existence.

The heart overcomes both objectivity and passivity. Because it is Pascal's recovery of the human from the distortions of the detached and disembodied mind, the heart is the repudiation of the "objective" morally neutral stance of the scientist. The heart opens the human being to something outside the closed circle of self-consciousness, to something greater than himself which can fill the emptiness he feels in the modern world, for the heart is open to the experience of mystery which allows Pascal to move from understanding to faith. Therefore, Pascal's account of human being is an articulation of the knowledge which comes through the rightly ordered heart.

Pascal's own existence becomes a question for him in the very activity of his own thought: "Man is only a reed, the weakest in nature, but he is a thinking reed. There is no need for the whole universe to take up arms to crush him: a vapor, a drop of water is enough to kill him. But even if the universe were to crush him, man would still be nobler than his slayer, because he knows that he is dying and the advantage the universe has over him. The universe knows none of this. Thus all our dignity consists in thought" (P, #200). Note that he does not attribute the nobility of man to his knowledge of or mastery over nature. Nor does he appeal, as philosophers and theologians do, to the immaterial nature of thought to prove the immortality of the soul. On the contrary, he refers to the fact that man knows he is dying. By focusing on his knowledge of death, he points to the embodiment and the mortality of the thinking reed and the powerlessness of man in the face of death.

Pascal's "reflexive consciousness," his mind reflecting on its own activity, comes to terms with the radical contingency of his own existence.[10] His reflection brings him more deeply into the lived reality of the "thinking reed" in its experience of facing death. "I feel that it is possible that I might never have existed, *for* my self consists in my thought, ... *therefore* I am not a necessary being. I am not eternal or infinite either" (P, #135, emphasis added). He feels the possibility of his never having existed.

Throughout this reflection on himself, Pascal emphasizes "feeling." He is speaking in the language of the heart, not in the terms of scientific objectivity. Pascal is addressing the detachment and indifference of modern consciousness, and forcing the searching mind to confront its anxiety. "When I consider the brief span of my life absorbed into the eternity which comes before and after ... the small space I occupy and which I see swallowed up in the infinite immensity of spaces of which I know nothing and which know nothing of me, I take fright and am amazed to see myself here rather than there; there is no reason for me to be here rather than there, now rather than then. Who put me here? By whose command and act were this time and place allotted to me?" (P, #68) Indeed, when he sees himself poised above the abysses of infinity and nothingness shown to him by modern science, he is "terrified at himself" (P, #199). He feels the radical contingency of his own particular existence, his own time and place, and his own particular existence is now a question for him. This is no longer merely a philosophical question about human nature. Rather it is the urgent question of his own being and his own death.

Man, then, is a misfit. His power of thought takes him, in some sense, outside of nature and frees him from nature: he knows what nature can never know. Yet, that same power of thought shows him that he is merely a reed, the weakest of all reeds, and that he going to die. So, he cannot make

---

[10] Georges Poulet, *Studies in Human Time*, trans. Elliott Coleman (Baltimore, MD: The Johns Hopkins Press, 1956), 81, 83.

sense of his own existence. Within this awareness of his own strangeness is hidden a desire for life, and within that instinctual desire for life is hidden his desire for eternal life. Hence, his fright, anxiety, and terror. This is the beginning of the heart's search for completeness.

Man's displacement makes him a monster and a freak. Man "is a monster that surpasses all understanding" (P, #130). Pascal uses this awareness of monstrosity to heighten the sense of darkness and anxiety. "Here is a strange monster, and a very palpable aberration. Here he is, fallen from his place, looking anxiously for it. That is what all men do" (P, #477). The contradiction between the greatness and the wretchedness of man points to a strange absence, a strange insufficiency in his nature and the need for transcendence of that nature: "What sort of freak then is man! How novel, how monstrous, how chaotic, how paradoxical, how prodigious! Judge of all things, feeble earthworm, repository of truth, sink of doubt and error, glory and refuse of the universe! Who will unravel such a tangle? This is certainly beyond dogmatism and skepticism, beyond all human philosophy. Man transcends man.... Know then, proud man, what a paradox you are to yourself.... Man infinitely transcends man.... Let us learn our true nature from the uncreated and incarnate truth" (P, #131).

The awareness of displacement leads the searching heart to the realization that nothing within his own nature can remedy his condition of contradiction and incompleteness. Neither can he be satisfied in the achievement of self-consciousness, the "inner transcendence" effected in the spiritualization of the incarnation. We see in the character of Rayber a man who, in spite of his pretention to self-containment, is deeply divided within himself, keeping himself upright on the very narrow line between madness and emptiness. And Hulga, who sees through everything to nothing, is really empty within herself. The Misfit, however, is aware of his displacement and, in his own way, he recognizes his need for transcendence. For he knows that there is something wrong with him and, instinctively, he understands that only faith in Christ can heal him.

Pascal concludes that the mystery of original sin is the only way to make sense of man's true condition. We cannot understand ourselves without recourse to this mystery: "For without it, what are we to say man is? His whole state depends on this imperceptible point" (P, #695). The imperceptible point is the instant of transmission of Adam's sin, an idea that shocks human reason. "It is an astounding thing that the mystery furthest from our ken, that of the transmission of sin, should be something without which we can have no knowledge of ourselves.... Certainly nothing jolts us more than this doctrine, and yet, but for this mystery, the most incomprehensible of all, we remain incomprehensible to ourselves. The knot of our condition was twisted and turned in that abyss, so that it is harder to conceive of man without this mystery than for man to conceive of it himself" (P, #131). The mystery of original sin shocks us because it seems so unjust. How can an individual be guilty and thus be punished for an offense that he himself did not commit, that he inherited from his father? This is what The Misfit sees so clearly.

Because God intends to make the mystery of our existence unintelligible to us, he "hid the knot so high, or more precisely, so low, that we were quite unable to reach it." Thus it is not through proud reason but through humble submission that we can really know ourselves (P, #131). The lowliness of the knot consists in the apparent transmission of original sin through the sexual act, the most lowly and common act of all animal nature.[11] The origin of our own condition is hidden in the lowliness of our biological origin.

In Pascal's grasp of man's incompleteness we can draw out what is perhaps the most fundamental difference between Pascal and Montaigne. The natural instinct and desire for eternal life is precisely what Montaigne

---

11   Hibbs, *Wagering*, 35: "In the case of Christianity, what seems lower is in fact higher. There is a note of comic reversal here. Such a reversal of expectation is also evident in the mode of revelation of the doctrine of original sin, the doctrine that explains the paradoxical duality of the human condition."

wants to overcome and suppress with his nonchalance about death and his satisfaction with the temporal. Montaigne wants man to be merely man. Like Montaigne, Pascal directs us to the goodness of "life itself." But, whereas for Montaigne, "life itself" means "this life," this temporal life of becoming, for Pascal the instinct for life, the meaning of "life itself," is eternal life. For Pascal, "this infinite abyss," this most fundamental desire for eternal life, "can be filled only with an infinite and immutable object, in other words by God himself" (P, #148). The "thinking reed" knows that it is going to die. Pascal's deep reflection is motivated by anxiety. He sees in man "an unsettling emptiness no worldly object could ever fill," and thus "man's radical inability to make himself whole."[12]

Pascal sees in Montaigne's account of the human condition the attempt to suppress the human desire for the transcendence of temporal existence.[13] Benjamin and Jenna Storey, in their explication of the meaning of modern "restlessness," argue that "in Pascal, the restlessness that is truly modern—the restlessness of the soul that tries and fails to hold itself within the confines of immanence—finds its first and most powerful voice."[14] The world of modern physics is silent in the face of man's questions about how he should live in that world. "The Montaignean quest for immanent contentment … takes place in the context of a universe that science relentlessly demonstrates to be no home for man. Truly thinking scientific modernism through intensifies rather than blunts our need for transcendence."[15] The recognition of our need for transcendence is the recognition of our need for a Redeemer. The mystery of original sin points to "the supreme mystery of the Passion and Redemption" (P, #560). Original sin is the source of our wretchedness, but it is also the occasion for the greatest manifestation of God's love.

---

12 McCarthy, "Pascal on Certainty and Utility," 106.
13 Hibbs, *Wagering*, 106.
14 Storey and Storey, *Why We Are Restless*, 52.
15 Storey and Storey, 55.

"Wretchedness induces despair. Pride induces presumption. The Incarnation shows man the greatness of his wretchedness through the greatness of the remedy required" (*P*, #352).

Pascal sees that Montaigne's immanent contentment is a kind of self-deception. Romano Guardini paints a picture of this Montaignean anthropology which Pascal rejects: "According to it, man would be by his body an element of nature, he would stand under its powers and be subject to them. The mind, however, would be rooted in itself and as such would be removed from nature. It could even, by thought, raise itself up in the face of nature and contain it. It would thus be greater than nature. It would find its center and footing in its own essence, and absolutely stated, it would by its own force be able to remain victorious even in its own destruction." Although the individual would feel lost in his insignificance and smallness in the boundless universe, he would, by the force of his mind alone, be able to rise above the limits of his nature. Thus, "we would have the ethic of heroic finiteness, which does indeed constitute one of the fundamental traits of the modern period at the threshold of its maturity."[16]

Guardini points to the difference between Pascal's conception of man and the modern conception of man as autonomous and self-sufficient. For Pascal, this modern self-sufficient man does not really exist. "The claim that there is such a man has only been able to be maintained through a tacit agreement of general self-deception; through a demonically consistent renunciation of the real greatness of man." In reality, however, man can only be fully man "if he dares to be more than 'man'—but turned towards God."[17] Pascal shows us that the necessity of transcending himself is precisely the most profound nature of man, and that "the refusal of this self-transcendence, as expressed in the idea of a self-sufficient nature,

---

16   Guardini, *Pascal*, 61–62.
17   Guardini, *Pascal*, 75.

whether naturalistic or humanistic, individualistic or collectivistic—thus means precisely the destruction of man's most essential nature."[18]

The "ethic of heroic finiteness" captures the meaning of Montaigne's (and Rayber's and Hulga's) modern consciousness, a consciousness achieved in the spiritualization and internalization of the meaning of the incarnation. Pascal shows us that man's transcendence of man cannot be understood as an ascent to the abstractions of spiritualization but only as the descent to the incarnate redeemer. We can learn our true nature only from the incarnate truth.

Like Pascal, O'Connor recognizes the limits of modern science for the study of man. She approaches the recovery of the reality of the incarnation through the restoration of the sense of mystery in the face of modern science which has no place for the mysteriousness of man. The modern secular world which does not believe in the fall, redemption, and judgment is the background for her stories: "The Liberal approach is that man has never fallen, never incurred guilt, and is ultimately perfectible by his own efforts. Therefore, evil in this light is a problem of better housing, sanitation, health, etc. and all mysteries will eventually be cleared up. Judgment is out of place because man is not responsible. Of course there are degrees of adherence to this, all sorts of mixtures, but it is the direction the modern heads toward" (*HB*, 302–3). This denial of the need for redemption is fostered by the belief that modern science can account fully for human being and that the science of psychology can make the human being his own savior.

O'Connor's appraisal of the effects of psychoanalysis points to what is lost in the search for self-consciousness. Referring to a friend who is struggling with the idea of entering the church but whose "conversion is still in the top of his head," she writes: "I would be afraid that a psychiatrist would make him lose the little he's gained, unless it was one who respected

---

18 Guardini, *Pascal*, 74.

his beliefs." And writing about a friend who has been treated by a psychiatrist, she expresses her concern: "When the psychiatrist got through with her, her emotions flowed magnificently and she believes nothing and herself is her God.... She is charming and very generous but headed for some major crack-up if she doesn't somehow get back some of what she lost in the psychiatrist's office" (*HB*, 427). Set against the background of the pervasive psychoanalytic attitude, O'Connor's task as a novelist might be described as the recovery of what is lost in the psychiatrist's office. "Herself is her God." What is lost is the mystery of the true meaning of redemption and our need for redemption.

O'Connor explains how the disappearance of the sense of mystery occurred. Since the sixteenth century, with the rise of modern science, the culture has been increasingly dominated by secular thought (*MM*, 185). And since the Enlightenment of the eighteenth century, which carried forward the promises of early modern science, "the popular spirit of each succeeding generation has tended more and more to the view that the mysteries of life will eventually fall before the mind of man" (*MM*, 158). In particular, modern man believes that the science of psychology can account fully for human being and that the practice of psychoanalysis is able eventually to make him whole. Against the background of this pervasive confidence in psychology, O'Connor brings out the mystery of human existence.

Although she recognizes the limited value of psychoanalysis, O'Connor warns of the danger it poses for religion. The modern world is divided about mystery, "part of it trying to eliminate mystery while another part tries to rediscover it in disciplines less personally demanding than religion" (*MM*, 145). Her criticisms of psychology concern Jung's reduction of mystery to symbols and thus his substitution of psychoanalysis for religion: "Jung has something to offer religion but is at the same time very dangerous for it. Jung would say, for instance, that Christ did not rise from the dead literally but we must realize that we need this symbol, that the notion has significance for our lives symbolically" (*HB*, 362–63). In a letter to a friend, she recounts the story of her visit with Mary McCarthy, who had left the church and had written a book about her Catholic upbringing. When the topic of conversation turned to the Eucharist, McCarthy said that she now thought of the Eucharist as a useful symbol. O'Connor replied: "Well, if it's a symbol, to hell with it" (*HB*, 125).

By transforming the historical realities of original sin, the incarnation, and the resurrection into symbolic meanings and by reducing the sacraments to symbols, Jung "spiritualizes" these historical and embodied realities. By reducing the Christian mysteries to symbols, psychology and psychoanalysis offer to those attempting to rediscover mystery the substitute for religion that O'Connor warns about. The need for the religious attitude suggests that man longs for something greater than himself, for the being who is the source of his life, but the symbols which Jung finds manifested in the dreams of his patients are merely the psychic realities which populate the "collective unconscious." Psychoanalysis is the process by which the individual recognizes and responds to these religious symbols, freeing himself from the biological forces of his subhuman nature. O'Connor's way into modern consciousness is through the sense of mystery because only the realization of the mystery of our existence can break through this closed circle of inner experience to historical reality, transcending the limits of the psychological.

O'Connor describes this mystery in several ways: the mystery of "existence" (*MM*, 133), of "incompleteness" (*MM*, 167), of "personality" (*MM*, 90), and of "human freedom" (*WB*, Author's Note). The central mystery around which all of these expressions revolve is the ultimate mystery of original sin and redemption. Drama, she says, is based on the bedrock of original sin (*MM*, 167). O'Connor's artfulness in presenting the mystery of sin and redemption will be discussed in chapter 5. Here, I want to emphasize O'Connor's insistence on the inadequacy of modern science, and of psychology in particular, for providing a complete account of human action.

The novelist must enlarge his field of vision beyond the human in order to begin to capture the meaning of human being, for those who reduce everything to human proportions eventually lose even the sense of the human itself (*HB*, 299–300). It is impossible to understand the human being apart from the mystery of his relationship to God. "The Catholic writer, insofar as he has the mind of the Church, will feel life from the standpoint of the central Christian mystery: that it has, for all its horror, been found by God to be worth dying for. But this should enlarge, not narrow, his field of vision" (*MM*, 146).

The field of vision must be enlarged because the modern mind tends to believe that everything about a character can be understood and explained in the terms of psychology, that the meaning of the character's actions will always be understandable in terms of the psychic forces at work within him. Up to a point, psychology and sociology can explain human behavior in terms of the psychic, unconscious forces that are the typical motivations of human conduct. However, O'Connor writes, "as for fiction, the meaning of a piece of fiction only begins where everything psychological and sociological has been explained" (*HB*, 299–300).

No good story could ever be limited to psychological and sociological explanations. The serious fiction writer knows that any story that can be entirely explained by the adequate motivation of its characters is not large enough. "The meaning of [a] story does not begin except at a depth where these things have been exhausted. The fiction writer presents mystery through manners, grace through nature, but when he finishes there always has to be left over that sense of Mystery which cannot be accounted for by any human formula" (*MM*, 153). In fiction "everything that has an explanation has to have it and the residue is Mystery with a capital M" (*HB*, 199).

When the fiction writer presents grace through nature, nature can be displayed in ways that are amenable to scientific explanation, but behind that display stands the mystery of original sin. That is what leaves the opening for the manifestations of the action of grace. It is only the sense of the mystery of divine grace that can take us out of ourselves to reality because mystery takes us beyond the predictable psychic events. Mystery is displayed by the author and encountered by the reader when the character breaks through the bonds of the psychological in response to the offering of grace.

Here the writer must confront "the clinical bias, the prejudice that sees everything strange as a case study in the abnormal" (MM, 165). But for O'Connor, in spite of a superficial sense of what is normal, we are all freaks, all displaced, all abnormal, on account of original sin. The writer "does not consider his characters any more freakish than ordinary fallen man usually is, [although] his audience is going to" (MM, 43). Like Pascal, she sees the freak as "a figure for our essential displacement" (MM, 45). And this displacement must be revealed against the background of this pervasive clinical bias. In particular, sin and evil must not be reduced to morally neutral psychic impulses. O'Connor says: "I want to be certain that the Devil gets identified as the Devil and not simply taken for this or that psychological tendency" (HB, 360).

In all of her stories, the mystery of the incarnation is made visible in the decision that the characters must make in the face of the reality of this unique historical intervention. The Misfit understands that the incarnation demands that a choice be made. Grace is offered and either accepted or rejected. The Misfit, that spoiled prophet-freak, in spite of his rejection of grace, has a much more profound understanding of his condition than does the head-doctor at the penitentiary: The Misfit knows that his guilt cannot be washed away through the process of psychotherapy.

For the psychotherapist, the beginning of psychoanalysis is found in its prototype, the confessional, for the very idea of sin leads to repressions which place a burden of guilt in the unconscious. By becoming conscious of concealed impulses, we mitigate the harm of repression, but if we conceal these impulses from ourselves, the harm cannot be corrected (*MMSS*, 31). Guilt is overcome in the process of achieving self-consciousness.

In *God and the Unconscious*, Victor White contrasts the meaning of confession in the sacrament of Penance with its meaning in psychoanalysis: "The confession required of the penitent and the confession required of the analysant are two very different things," for the analyst is concerned with the misdeeds of his patient not as moral offences but as causes or symptoms of neurosis. A confessor, on the other hand, "is required to act as *judge* of the objective moral rightness or wrongness of what is told to him, ... [But] an analyst has no like authority to pronounce moral judgments, and for therapeutic reasons will usually refuse resolutely to do so."[19]

As Jung insists, throughout the process of psychic healing, the psychoanalyst must never pass judgment on the patient but must maintain "an attitude of unprejudiced objectivity" (*MMSS*, 234). Unprejudiced objectivity, then, requires the suspension of all moral "prejudices." The psychotherapist "must have no fixed ideas as to what is right and wrong, nor must he pretend to know what is right and what is not—otherwise he takes something from the richness of the [psychoanalytical] experience" (*MMSS*, 239). Psychoanalysis has no place for contrition and repentance. Romano Guardini argues that because the human being is more than his psycho-physical being, "mere psychiatry" is not able to heal the sinner. "He would have to undergo conversion. This conversion could not be accomplished by a mere act of the will. It would have to consist in a true change of heart, and it would be more difficult than any therapeutic treatment."[20]

---

19   Victor White, OP, *God and the Unconscious* (Cleveland, OH and New York: Meridian Books, The World Publishing Company, 1961), 183–84.

20   Romano Guardini, *The World and the Person and Other Writings*, trans. Stella Lange (Washington, DC: Regnery Gateway, 2023), 337.

In *The Concept of Sin*, Josef Pieper warns that "psychotherapeutic theory and praxis propagate influential misunderstandings." He recounts the story of his visit with a highly regarded psychotherapist who told him that hearing confession of sins was his full-time job. Pieper could not suppress his astonishment and asked the smug psychiatrist whether he had the competence to say to his patients: "I absolve you from your sins." Because it is a decision against God, sin "can really only be extinguished by one act, by one act alone: the gift of forgiveness freely bestowed on us by God himself."[21] O'Connor leaves open the possibility that The Misfit, conscious of his sins, will ask for the forgiveness that only Christ can give.

---

21   Josef Pieper, *The Concept of Sin*, trans. Edward T. Oakes, SJ (South Bend, IN: St. Augustine's Press, 2001), 96–97.

5. O'Connor's Comic Art of the Possible and Pascal's True Philosophy

O'Connor's art and Pascal's philosophy are addressed to a modern audience. Pascal finds that in the modern world "there are only three sorts of people: those who have found God and serve him; those who are busy seeking him and have not found him; those who live without either seeking or finding him. The first are reasonable and happy, the last are foolish and unhappy, those in the middle are unhappy and reasonable" (*P*, #160). He makes "an absolute distinction between those who strive with all their might to learn and those who live without troubling themselves or thinking about it." Such "supernatural torpor" is "a monstrous thing." Only two classes of persons can be called reasonable: "those who serve God with all their heart because they know him and those who seek him with all their heart because they do not know him" (*P*, #427). Of those unhappy people who seek God but have not found him Pascal says: "I can only approve of those who seek with groans" (*P*, #405).

Pascal's description of the indifferent individual points to the new modern man who intends to make himself complete in himself, having internalized and brought under his consciousness the religious impulses which would otherwise draw him out of himself to something greater than himself. He wants to make himself whole and content with this temporal life, eliminating the desire for eternal life, indifferent to the question of the meaning of his existence.

Three centuries after Pascal describes the indifferent and complacent audience of his day, O'Connor must address essentially the same kind of audience. What has changed over those three centuries is the success of the science of psychology in persuading the modern mind that it can adequately account for human being. What has been lost is any trace of the sense of mystery in the human being's attempt to understand himself and any sense of the need for transcendence of the purely human. What Pascal faced in its origins, O'Connor faces in its full effect.

In her essay "Novelist and Believer," she sets out her own version of the three types of modern man. The first type resembles Jung's truly modern individual: self-created, self-centered, and self-satisfied. He is the man who recognizes no being outside himself whom he can adore as his creator: he becomes his own ultimate concern, sees himself as the master of all things, has his own sense of dignity and pride, and is satisfied within himself. The second is the type who does recognize a being outside himself but does not believe that this being can be known or approached. This seems to be the type who might recognize the religious impulse within himself but has "domesticated [his] despair and learned to live with it happily." Both are closed to the mystery of their own existence.

Susan Srigley elaborates on the first and second types. In the first type, "the spiritual experience is drawn wholly into the human, initiated and exhausted in its meaning by human needs and ends." In the second type, "an external, divine being is seen as separate from the human and, because of this separation, is ultimately unable to penetrate human life and be known sacramentally in the world." These are two examples of what O'Connor calls "spiritually lopsided" modern tendencies.[1]

O'Connor's third type is the modern man who "can neither believe nor contain himself in unbelief and who searches desperately, feeling about in all experience for the lost God" (*MM*, 159). O'Connor says that when the religious need is banished, the sense of mystery vanishes. However, "the searchers are another matter. Pascal wrote in his notebook, 'If I had not known you, I would not have found you'" (*MM*, 160). The searcher is open to finding Christ because in some way he already knows him. The searcher, then, is the type of human being who may be open to the experience of mystery which she captures in her stories. Her task as a novelist is to display the mystery of human life in a way that might be visible to "the kind of mind that is willing to have its sense of mystery deepened by contact with reality, and its sense of reality deepened by contact with mystery" (*MM*, 79).

In her correspondence with a young man who is struggling with the possibility of entering the church, O'Connor writes: "I hope you'll find the experience you need to make the leap toward Christianity seem the only one to you. Pascal had a good deal to say about this" (*HB*, 485). It would have to be an *experience*, not an argument, that would make the leap possible. O'Connor's task as a novelist is to create the *experience* of the *possibility* of grace.[2]

---

[1] Susan Srigley, *Flannery O'Connor's Sacramental Art* (Notre Dame, IN: University of Notre Dame Press, 2004), 21.

[2] In focusing on the metaphysical category of possibility, O'Connor does indeed remain in the spirit of the Thomistic tradition. Aquinas is very clear that reason cannot prove the articles of faith, but it can remove obstacles to faith and thus show that what is proposed for our belief is "not impossible." Thomas Aquinas, *Summa Theologica*, trans. Fathers of the English Dominican Province, 5 vols. (Notre Dame, IN: Ave Maria, Christian Classics, 1981), Second Part of Part Two, Question 2, Article 10, Reply to Second Objection: "The reasons which are brought forward

In her Author's Note to the second edition of *Wise Blood*, O'Connor describes *Wise Blood* as a comic novel: "It is a comic novel about a Christian *malgre lui*, and as such, very serious, for all comic novels that are any good must be about matters of life and death." Marion Montgomery explains that O'Connor's work is properly called comedy in Dante's sense: the possibility of grace and redemption is always offered. The denouement of her stories "restores spiritual contingency" for the modern world.[3]

While O'Connor recognizes the greatness of Dante's poetry, she realizes that, in the modern world, Dante's approach could not succeed:

> I am often told that the model of balance for the novelist should be Dante, who divided his territory up pretty evenly between hell, purgatory and paradise. There can be no objection to this, but also there can be no reason to assume that the result of doing it in these times will give us the balanced picture that it gave in Dante's. Dante lived in the thirteenth century, when that balance was achieved in the faith of his age. We live now in an age which doubts both fact and value, which is swept this way and that by momentary convictions. Instead of reflecting a balance from the world around him, the novelist now has to achieve one from a felt balance inside himself. (*MM*, 49)

In the middle of his temporal life, Dante is taken into eternal life, into the "other world," descending into the depths of hell, then ascending the

---

in support of the authority of faith are not demonstrations which can bring intellectual vision to the human intellect; and so the unseen is not removed. But they remove obstacles to faith, by showing that what faith proposes is not impossible." However, O'Connor's way is not through argument and reason but fiction and imagination. And her audience is not the medieval Christian of the thirteenth century but the modern man searching for truth in a culture that is closed to the possibility of the transcendent and of eternal life.

3 Montgomery, *Innerleckchuls*, 17.

mount of purgatory, and finally ascending to the heights of heaven and the contemplation of the divine. The modern fiction writer, however, must descend into himself, into the darkness of the familiar. The felt balance within must be achieved in this specifically modern way. The modern reader must be given a glimpse of the other world while remaining in this world. Dante's pilgrim becomes O'Connor's prophet-freak.

The medieval approach to the most fundamental questions of human life cannot be effective in the modern world because the modern audience is so different from Dante's fourteenth-century readers. Given her indifferent and skeptical audience, which does not believe in eternity or any "other world," O'Connor must accomplish everything in this world, in her own time and place. To restore spiritual contingency is to take the way of the possible, bringing out the possible in the actual. Her way is not to ascend to paradise but to descend to the most concrete details of the here and now in this world: she looks through the common, familiar, and ordinary to the mystery of redemption. As she records in her journal, her prayer is: "Please help me to get down under things and find where You are" (*PJ*, 4).

William Lynch, in *Christ and Apollo: The Dimensions of the Literary Imagination*, describes the "descent" which is characteristic of comedy: "It gets below all the categories within which the most of life is spent and destroys the most of these categories (the rich, the proud, the mighty, the beautiful . . .) in its descent. In this descent it discovers a kind of rock-bottom reality in man . . . which is profoundly and funnily unbreakable, which has no needs above itself. It seems to be the most inherently confident rung of the finite. It is ugly *and* strong. . . . Things are really funny—because wonderful realities can come of their lowermost depths."[4]

In contrast with tragedy, comedy requires "more faith in the finite, the pure finite," for "in tragedy there is always a little danger that the very size of the abyss will hide its finitude, the very heroicity of the depth

---

4   Lynch, *Christ and Apollo*, 113.

will conceal its littleness." In the face of the finite, comedy is completely unblinking, without deception, and faces the actual with a great form of courage, "the courage of the comic."[5] Comedy is the reminder that "it is the limited concrete which is the path to insight and salvation."[6]

While tragedy concerns characters who are somewhat "above" us, comedy concerns those who are "below" us. Tragedy demands "the inviolable primacy of the noble type."[7] O'Connor's characters, however, are almost always from the lowest stratum of social life. Who could be more lowly on the social scale than the poor, white, backwoods Southern characters who appear in her stories? Yet her fiction is not comic in the sense of mockery and ridicule of the lowly. She identifies herself with her backwoods prophets and freaks. Her characters are not "noble" in the classical Aristotelian sense, yet they do attain a kind of nobility in their integrity. O'Connor shows us the action of the divine in the most common and lowly, for in the most important sense, we are all the most common and lowly. The "prophet-freak" of her stories is only the image of herself (*MM*, 118).

In choosing her characters from the most lowly, O'Connor is confronting directly the sense of intellectual superiority of Hulga and Rayber. The nature of comedy, with the lowliness of its characters, is the clearest and most forceful way to display the mystery of salvation because it makes it much more difficult to confuse the action of grace with any kind of natural or acquired intellectual superiority or social, economic, or even moral worthiness. Clearly, grace is an entirely free gift, not merited in any way by the character. Indeed, the very lowliness and banality of her characters leave no room for doubt about the unworthiness of the recipient or the absolute generosity of the giver. If the possibility of grace can be seen in

---

5   Lynch, 117.
6   Lynch, 121.
7   Jones, *On Aristotle and Greek Tragedy* (New York: Oxford University Press, 1962), 57.

the comic and the most lowly, then the reality of that possibility is established firmly on the lowest rung of the natural and conventional hierarchy. It is in this vision of the highest in the lowest that comedy directly confronts the separation of spirit and matter.

O'Connor's fiction is "an incarnational art" (*MM*, 68), and the essence of her fiction is the embodiment of mystery (*MM*, 129). Art is incarnational because it embodies mystery. O'Connor says that the "modern spirit" is to separate spirit and matter (*MM*, 68). She insists, however, that "when the physical fact is separated from the spiritual reality, the dissolution of belief is eventually inevitable" (*MM*, 162). Fiction overcomes this separation: a novel should lead the reader to "contemplation of the mystery embodied in it" (*MM*, 129). Mystery, then, is not experienced through a separation of spirit and matter, as something purely spiritual. O'Connor quotes Baron von Hügel: "the Supernatural experience always appears as the transfiguration of Natural conditions, acts, states.... The Spiritual generally is always preceded, or occasioned, accompanied or followed, by the Sensible.... The highest realities and deepest responses are experienced by us within, or in contact with, the lower and lowliest" (*MM*, 176). The good novelist knows that "he cannot approach the infinite directly, that he must penetrate the natural human world as it is" (*MM*, 163). The visible makes possible the *revelation* of the hidden.

How is the invisible revealed in O'Connor's stories? Adapting Aristotle's definition of art, we might say that fiction is "an imitation of action." O'Connor says that "a story is a complete dramatic action" (*MM*, 90) and in "a complete story, ... the action fully illuminates the meaning" (*MM*, 102). The "action" of a story must be distinguished from its plot. The plot is the narrative, the sequence of deeds and words of the characters in the story. We see the plot but we do not see the action, for the action is not the same as the visible deeds of the plot. Yet, the action is "embodied" in the plot: the plot makes it possible for us to see the invisible action.

In O'Connor's stories, the action is always the offering of grace and the free acceptance or rejection of grace. The action is always both divine and human, and the meaning of the action is always the possibility of the characters' participation in the divine life. O'Connor's stories display the possibility of action for the modern man against the background of his psychological pushes and pulls. A good story could never be limited to the interplay of merely psychological "forces."

O'Connor must display the possibility of grace against the background of the pervasive psychological attitude toward human conduct. In her incarnational artistry, the plot—all of the deeds and words of the characters—leads up to that moment in time when the choice must be made, the moment in which grace is offered. In order to see grace, you have to see change, and that requires a narrative which moves through time. The working out of that possibility of change in the lives of individuals requires time and the effecting of change at the deepest level of the personality, the level of freedom and choice, beyond the limits of the psychological.

The Catholic novel "cannot see man as determined; it cannot see him as totally depraved. It will see him as incomplete in himself, as prone to evil, but as redeemable when his own efforts are assisted by grace. And it will see this grace as working through nature, but as entirely transcending it, so that a door is always open to possibility and the unexpected in the human soul. Its center of meaning will be Christ" (*MM*, 196–97). In her stories, the plot always sets up the moment in which the characters confront the possible and must choose in that context.

Since grace itself is not visible, O'Connor says that "it's almost impossible to write about supernatural Grace in fiction" (*HB*, 144). The presence of grace is revealed and can be seen only in its action on the character. And its action on the character must be somehow in keeping with the nature of that particular character. Fiction shows "the presence of grace as it appears in nature" (*MM*, 147). Indeed, it is impossible to show the operation of grace when grace is cut off from nature (*MM*, 166). The character's encounter with God is an experience which is both natural and supernatural. It is this experience which the writer must make understandable and credible to his reader (*MM*, 161). Therefore, "the more a writer wishes to make the supernatural apparent, the more real he has to be able to make the natural world" (*MM*, 116). In order to make the experience credible, he must make the supernatural action of grace fit the nature of the character even though grace changes the character in a fundamental way. It is "the moment of grace [which] makes a story work" (*HB*, 465).

O'Connor explains how she approaches the meaning of her stories and the moment of grace which makes them work. "The writer whose point of view is Catholic in the widest sense of the term reads nature the same way the medieval commentators read Scripture. They found three levels of meaning in the literal level of the sacred text—the allegorical, in which one thing stands for another; the moral, which has to do with what should be done; and the anagogical, which has to do with the Divine life and our participation in it, the level of grace" (*HB*, 468–69). Here she is paraphrasing Aquinas who asks whether in Holy Scripture a word may have several senses. Aquinas explains that God can "signify his meaning, not by words only (as man also can do), but also by things themselves." In Sacred Scripture, "the first signification whereby words signify things belongs to the first sense, the historical or literal." The way in which things themselves have a signification is called the "spiritual sense." This spiritual sense, it should be emphasized, is not "abstracted" from the literal historical meaning but is "based on the literal, and presupposes it." There can be no separation of the spiritual from the historical realities.

The spiritual sense in which things themselves have significance is threefold. First, the allegorical sense refers to the way the things of the Old Law signify the things of the New Law. Abraham's sacrifice of Isaac, for example, prefigures the sacrifice of Christ. Both are historical events, but the actions of Abraham can be fully understood only insofar as they are seen in light of the actions of Christ. Second, the moral sense is the way in which the things done in Christ are "signs of what we ought to do." Again, the spiritual moral sense cannot be separated or abstracted from the historical events of the life of Christ. Third, the anagogical sense is the sense in which things themselves signify "what relates to eternal glory." Aquinas insists that "all of the senses are founded on one—the literal."[8]

In O'Connor's art, the spiritual is never separated from the literal. Her primary focus is anagogical signification having to do with the action of grace and our participation in the divine life in this world. In her review of Lynch's *Christ and Apollo*, O'Connor explains that this form of scriptural exegesis, when applied to nature, is the "thorough penetration of the limited … a way which leaves open the most possibilities to be found in the actual" (*Pres*, 94). The thorough penetration of the limited allows the full meaning of the reality embodied in the concrete to appear in the act of prophetic vision. This reality appears as a "possibility" within the actual, so that the reader can see the moment of grace, not as inevitable, but as the appearance of the unexpected in which he catches a glimpse of the eternal in time. In this description of her vision as the opening up of possibilities within the moment, we see the way in which O'Connor allows a glimpse of the eternal for the modern mind which is closed to the possibility of eternal life.

For O'Connor, anagogical signification is the way through the common and familiar to mystery. As Peter Candler explains, "the logic of anagogy implies that the visible realities of this world only take on a fullness of meaning—indeed, they only become truly *visible*—when seen in the paradoxical light of the unseen." The anagogical imagination does not remove the individual from this world. Rather the anagogical sense "leads one through the contemplation of future glory to the reimagination of temporal existence in light of the Incarnation." When seen in the light of

---

8   Aquinas, *Summa Theologica*, Part One, Question 1, Article 10.

divine glory, "the world—including most especially humanity—becomes more truly visible for what it is."[9]

Anagogical vision is O'Connor's prophetic vision. Prophetic vision is not primarily or essentially a matter of foretelling the future. Anagogical vision is prophetic vision because "prophecy is a matter of seeing near things with their extensions of meaning and thus of seeing far things close up. The prophet is a realist of distances" (*MM*, 44). But what is the nature of the distances which prophetic vision encompasses? Anagogical vision is "the kind of vision that is able to see different levels of reality in one image or one situation" (*MM*, 72). The true meaning of a situation or action is not entirely on the surface. But it cannot be reached without first penetrating the surface, for its meaning is "embodied" in the concrete, interwoven with the texture of ordinary life. The surface reveals something of the depths at which the action is occurring. The prophet is a realist of distances because he sees the connection between the surface and the depth. This is "the prophetic sense of 'seeing through' reality" (*Conv*, 88–89).

The moment of grace is the moment in which the "anagogical level of action" takes place, the moment in which the agent experiences his participation in the divine life (*MM*, 204). And the vision which captures that action is prophetic vision. The anagogical-prophetic vision of the writer "operates at a peculiar crossroads where time and place and eternity somehow meet." The problem for the writer is to find that location (*MM*, 59).

What the anagogical-prophetic vision sees is embodied mystery. The writer looks for "one image that will connect or combine or embody two points; one is a point in the concrete, and the other is a point not visible to the naked eye, but believed in by him firmly, just as real to him, really, as the one that everybody sees" (*MM*, 42). Although the distances

---

9   Peter M. Candler Jr., "The Anagogical Imagination of Flannery O'Connor," *Christianity and Literature* 60, no. 1 (Autumn 2010): 12.

between these two points are "so great" (*MM*, 42), the writer must cover these distances with an image that can carry the meaning of the action. In "A Good Man is Hard to Find," the Grandmother touches the man who is about to shoot her. That touch is an image that connects the physical world with the moment of grace, a visible gesture which reveals a supernatural mystery.

The distance covered in anagogical-prophetic vision is the distance traveled in the act of faith. O'Connor says: "Dogma is the guardian of mystery. The doctrines are spiritually significant in ways that we cannot fathom. According to St. Thomas, prophetic vision is not a matter of seeing clearly, but of seeing what is distant, hidden" (*HB*, 365). The distance for prophetic vision is the distance from the surface to hiddenness, the hiddenness of mystery. The distance is that between the visible and the invisible, the temporal moment and eternity, human life and divine life. Eternal life is not in "the next world" but begins in this world. "Eternity begins in time and ... we must stop thinking about it as something that follows time" (*HB*, 171). Prophecy, for the writer, is not a matter of predicting the future. Rather it is a matter of seeing the eternal hidden in the present, the supernatural in the natural, the mystery in its embodiment.

That anagogical vision is the vision of embodied mystery is shown by the fact that O'Connor herself is surprised by what she makes in her attempt to be true to the reality of experience. "If a writer is any good, what he makes will have its source in a realm much larger than that which his conscious mind can encompass and will always be a greater surprise to him than it can ever be to his reader" (*MM*, 83). The limits of the conscious mind are revealed in the fact that she does not fully understand the experiences she writes about. Rather, she contemplates the experience and understands that she does not understand it. That is "the anagogical way of seeing" (*HB*, 180). She comments on her own favorite story: "I think it's one of the best stories I've written, and this is because there is a good deal more in it than I understand myself" (*HB*, 140). This experience of the revelation of mystery belongs not only to the Catholic or religious writer, but to all serious fiction writers who are attempting to be true to the concrete reality from which they begin. "I think that a serious fiction writer describes an action only in order to reveal a mystery. Of course, he may be revealing the mystery to himself at the same time he is revealing it to everyone else. He may not even succeed in revealing it to himself, but I think he must sense its presence at least" (*Conv*, 9). The fiction writer does not explain; he presents the action for contemplation.

What is the experience that the writer wants to make vivid in presenting his anagogical-prophetic vision? "In fiction … the hardest thing for the writer to indicate is the presence of the anagogical which to my mind is the only thing that can cause the personality to change" (*HB*, 503). The experience of this change of personality is the action where "the real heart of the story lies." That action must be "both totally right and totally unexpected," "both in character and beyond character," and it must suggest "both the world and eternity." An action of this kind would be on the "anagogical level," the level which has to do with the Divine life and our participation in it. It would be "a gesture which somehow made contact with mystery" (*MM*, 111). In the central action of "A Good Man Is Hard to Find," the Grandmother, recognizing the bonds of kinship, touches The Misfit. The Grandmother's gesture embodies the mystery for the reader to experience and contemplate, and that contemplation is deepened by the sense that, behind this story, is the story of the fall and redemption, Eve reaching out to her children.

O'Connor says that the searching mind "feels about in all experience for the lost God." Her task, then, is to create the *experience* of mystery and to bring out the *meaning* of that experience. For the reader, a story is "an experience of meaning" (*MM*, 94). For the fictional character, the *experience* is that of being offered grace and either accepting it or rejecting it: the experience of a choice, of a possibility suddenly being offered, the chance for a *free* act which would necessarily be a change at the deepest level of one's self. It is the experience of a free act but, at the same time, the experience of something given.

A meaningful story cannot be simply the narration of a series of events in which the same psychic forces produce the same kinds of effects in the characters. The story must have a meaningful action, the focal point around which everything turns. O'Connor says: "If there is no possibility for change in a character, we have no interest in him" (*HB*, 199). Because it is our participation in the very life of Christ, the presence of the anagogical is the only thing that can cause the personality to change. The change that occurs in her characters is an action at the deepest level, the level of the "personality," for personality is deeper than Jung's consciousness. Personality is a mystery, the mystery experienced in human freedom, which is not the same kind of freedom promised in psychoanalysis. The free act in which the personality changes occurs in the moment of grace, and the task of the writer is to make that moment, that free action, seem possible and credible. It must appear to be possible, not inevitable, for if it seems inevitable then we are still at the level of psychic forces.

O'Connor writes: "the meaning of a story does not begin except at a depth where adequate motivation and adequate psychology and the various determinations have been exhausted. [The] writer will be interested in what we don't understand rather than in what we do. He will be interested in possibility rather than in probability. He will be interested in characters who are forced out to meet evil and grace and who act on a trust beyond themselves" (*MM*, 41–42).

Even though the novelist writes about characters who are mostly unfree, "it is the free action, the open possibility," which illuminates and gives life to the story. O'Connor says: "It is the free act, the acceptance of grace particularly, that I always have my eye on" (*MM*, 115). This kind of freedom and change in a character is very difficult for the modern mind to recognize and accept as real. The writer, then, must make the moment of grace appear surprising but not unbelievable. For the change is not forced on the character from outside. Yet, at the same time, the change is not predictable. There is the possibility of either accepting or rejecting the grace that is offered. That is the choice that creates the tension of the story: "All human nature vigorously resists grace because grace changes us and the change is painful" (*HB*, 307). The change is painful because it amounts to a break with the psychic forces that resist such change. Will the character accept or reject the possibility of freedom that is offered to him in the moment of grace? As The Misfit, that "spoiled prophet," realizes, the incarnation, that unique intervention in human history, has made this choice inevitable.

Here we are at the deepest level of O'Connor's prophetic vision: to see the moment of grace and freedom is to see through the ordinary to the extraordinary, through the common to the uncommon. Her prophetic vision directly confronts the modern psychological prejudice, seeing through the familiarity of the psychological to the freedom which transcends it. Her focus is always on the moment of possibility and decision.

O'Connor recommends Pascal's philosophy as preparation for "the leap toward Christianity," the risk of the decision to follow Christ. Pascal's "true philosophy" is his disclosure of the possibility of faith in the modern world. We can bring out Pascal's specifically modern way of illuminating the possibility of faith by discussing more fully the contrast between his mode of thought and the mode of medieval theology which uses the categories and logic of classical philosophy. The content of faith is not different for the medieval believer and the modern believer. Rather, these are different ways of arriving at an understanding of the meaning of faith and of giving a philosophical account of the content of belief.

Consider, for example, the so-called ontological argument of St. Anselm's *Proslogion*. Anselm begins from faith: he asks God to help him to understand "that You are what we believe You to be."[10] From his belief in the greatness of God, Anselm moves through the logic of his argument to a deeper understanding of the mystery of God's greatness and to adoring contemplation of this divine eternal being. Pascal, on the other hand, begins not from faith but from experience of the moral life, and ends in the recognition of the divinity of the crucified Christ. Thus, his true philosophy does not ascend to the heights of contemplation of the eternal divine being but descends to the lowliness of the incarnation. He discovers the possibility of the highest in the lowest, the eternal in the temporal, the extraordinary in the familiar. Indeed, the mystery of the greatness of God illuminated in Anselm's theology is most perfectly manifested in the humility of the crucified Christ.

True philosophy sets out the experience of the human condition in the modern world and opens the modern mind to the possibility of the truth of the humiliated God revealed in the Gospels. In his recognition of the limits and inadequacy of modern science for the study of man, Pascal reveals both the radical nature of his critique of modern philosophy and the uniqueness of his own philosophical position. Pascal says: "To mock philosophy is to be a true philosopher" (P, #513). The philosophy which shows us our true condition "is certainly beyond dogmatism and skepticism, beyond all human philosophy. Man transcends man.... Let us learn our true nature from the uncreated and incarnate truth" (P, #131). Since the world "only exists through Christ, for Christ, and to teach men about their corruption and redemption" (P, #449), human philosophy cannot teach us about our true condition. True philosophy is beyond all human philosophy.

What, then, is Pascal's true philosophy and how is it beyond all human philosophy? Recall T. S. Eliot's description of Pascal's mode of thought:

---

10   St. Anselm, *Proslogion*, trans. M. J. Charlesworth (Notre Dame, IN: University of Notre Dame Press, 1979), 117.

Pascal looks at the moral world unflinchingly and concludes that, among all religions, only Christianity can make sense of our moral condition. Thus he finds himself convinced of the doctrine of the incarnation.

Josef Pieper, describing his own approach to the moral world, gives us a more complete picture of Pascal's mode of thought and the central role that possibility plays in his thought. His account of the philosophical practice of the believer captures what I take to be the procedure of Pascal's "true philosopher." Pieper describes the philosopher as one who considers a question "under every possible aspect." Like Pascal, he begins his inquiry into the meaning of human existence from the moral world, in particular from the phenomena of moral failure and guilt. What do these phenomena tell us about human being as such?

First, the philosopher considers the possibility that moral failure and guilt can be explained in purely human terms: moral failure as the violation of a moral code contrived by human beings and guilt as the psychological response of the troubled conscience (the position of Freud and Jung). On this account, there is no such thing as sin, that is, moral failing as an offense against God.

But the true philosopher who wants to consider the matter under every possibility, also has available to him the meaning of moral failure as it appears in revelation. The philosopher who is a believer is convinced that man's rejection of God has led to the immense historical events of the incarnation and redemption. Therefore, he cannot accept the claim that moral failure and guilt are exhaustively described as a violation of man-made rules of behavior or of societal "values."

Here, the philosopher must be prepared "to step into the shadow of mystery." He sees the phenomena of moral failure and human guilt in the light of a "transhuman truth," and arrives then at the "ground" of the phenomenon of human guilt.[11] The attempt to think through the meaning

---

11   Pieper, *Concept of Sin*, 13–14.

of guilt to its ground ends in the mystery of original sin, the mystery expressed as "inherited sin, which Pascal so well knew."[12] Revelation offers this mystery to the philosophical mind, a possibility which would not have been available without the historical fact of Christ's claim to be God incarnate: the nature of sin is such that it demands this remedy of the suffering and death of the Son of God.

However, because the truth of the incarnation is now a *possibility* for thought, it does not *compel* the assent of the human mind. We are brought, then, to the point where a choice must be made, a life-or-death decision to follow Christ or reject him. Throughout the *Pensées*, the urgency of the question of eternal life is pressed upon us and becomes explicit in the Wager where the analogy of gambling, with the stakes nothing less than eternity, is the perfect way to force the issue of decision and choice. Once the obstacles to faith have been removed and the possibility of eternal life has been shown, it is time to place your bets. Pascal sets up the situation in which "you must wager. There is no choice, you are already committed" (P, #418).

Romano Guardini describes the context in which the choice must be made. Because God is hidden, because of the "scandal" of the incarnation, "the essence of the situation of revelation consists in the fact that it brings about the possibility of hesitation.... Thus arises the psychological and intellectual sphere which is necessary in order for freedom to enter into the possibility of choice." It is at this moment that "the person accomplishes, from his own power of initiative, the movement of passage to the beyond, the self-surrender to the divine Thou," and either, in faith, accepts the offering of grace or rejects faith and turns in upon himself.[13] The act of judgment here takes place under the threat of the possibility of doubt. "This ultimate suspension is no longer overcome by an intrinsic clarity which the object forces upon one, but by an act of decision."[14]

---

12 Pieper, 77.
13 Guardini, *Pascal*, 127.
14 Guardini, 151.

But the searching mind objects: "I am so made that I cannot believe." Pascal replies: "if you are unable to believe, it is because of your passions, since reason impels you to believe and yet you cannot do so. Concentrate then not on convincing yourself by multiplying proofs of God's existence but by diminishing your passions." Pascal is addressing the man who wants to find faith and be cured of unbelief. Such a man should learn from those who were once "bound" in this way but who now wager all they have. "Follow the way by which they began. They behaved just as if they did believe, taking holy water, having Masses said, and so on. That will make you believe quite naturally, and will make you more docile ... this diminishes the passions." Pascal describes himself here as "a man who went down upon his knees" to submit his own being to the infinite being, to pray that the searching mind might be brought to submit his being to God, and "that strength might thus be reconciled with lowliness" (*P*, #418). Pascal's wager is not a metaphysical argument for the existence of God. He is not addressing the mind but the heart, encouraging the inquirer to open his heart to the possibility of grace, for faith is God perceived by the heart. In the act of wagering, the individual "acts on the basis of commitment to the *possibility* of the free gift of divine grace."[15]

The urgency of the decision, for both Pascal and O'Connor, is felt in the realization of the inevitability of death. O'Connor writes: "In every story there is some minor revelation which, no matter how funny the story may be, gives us a hint of the unknown, of death" (*Conv*, 17). Her

---

[15] Virgil Martin Nemoianu, "Pascalian Faith and the Place of the Wager," *The Heythrop Journal* 52, no. 1 (2011): 27. In his discussion of the meaning of Pascal's wager, Virgil Nemoianu explains that the will has two possible ultimate tendencies. The first is the tendency to the sovereignty of the human will: "One may will as if one's self were the central ordering principle of all things, as if the world and everything in it, including other selves, existed for one's exclusive acquisition, ownership, and use ... as though one were master and possessor of nature." Or one may will as though "God were the central ordering principle. Pascal describes this way of willing as the transformation or conversion of the particular will" (32).

characters are placed in those extreme situations that best reveal what we are essentially (*MM*, 113). In "A Good Man is Hard to Find," for example, the Grandmother, confronted with the man who is about to kill her, is placed in "the most significant position life offers the Christian. She is facing death" (*MM*, 110). But we are all always in that position, even though we refuse to think about it and thus almost never experience the urgency of the decision of faith. Fiction allows the writer to make the immediacy of our position real to us. When The Misfit, in his comic observation, says of the Grandmother that she would have been a good woman if there had been somebody there to shoot her every minute of her life, he shows us that O'Connor's stories focus the whole of life into that moment when the reality of death is inescapable, when grace is offered, so that the reader might understand that "the creative action of the Christian's life is to prepare his death in Christ" (*MM*, 223). For O'Connor, "the greatest dramas naturally involve the salvation or loss of the soul" (*MM*, 167).

In order to overcome the indifference of the modern mind to the fundamental questions of salvation and eternal life, the writer must make his vision apparent "by shock" and use "violent means to get his vision across to this hostile audience" (*MM*, 34). Commenting on the baptism at the center of *The Violent Bear It Away*, O'Connor says: "I know that for the larger percentage of my readers, baptism is a meaningless rite; therefore I have to imbue this action with an awe and terror which will suggest its awful mystery. I have to distort the look of the thing in order to represent as I see them both the mystery and the fact" (*Conv*, 88–89).

Violence returns her characters to reality, the reality and urgency of their true condition, forcing them out of complacency and indifference. "Reality is something to which we must be returned at considerable cost," the cost of a painful, fundamental change in one's life, for the need for this kind of change is "implicit in the Christian view of the world" (*MM*, 112). True, grace is healing, but the notion that grace is healing "omits the fact that before it heals, it cuts with the sword Christ said he came to bring"

(*HB*, 411). Violence can be used for good or evil, but "among other things taken by it is the kingdom of heaven" (*MM*, 113).

O'Connor interprets this passage—"the kingdom of heaven suffers violence and the violent bear it away"—as referring to "the violence of love" which she sees, for example, in the asceticism of John the Baptist and the Desert Fathers (*HB*, 382). Violence allows us to see the struggle between the natural, psychic events within the individual, and the offering of grace which transcends the natural. O'Connor says: "I am much more interested in the nobility of unnaturalness than in the nobility of naturalness.... It is the business of the artist to uncover the strangeness of truth. The violent are not natural. St. Thomas's gloss on this verse is that the violent [whom] Christ is here talking about represent those ascetics who strain against mere nature. St. Augustine concurs. I will take just as much naturalness as I need to accomplish my purposes, no more, but a Freudian could read this novel [*The Violent Bear It Away*] and explain it all on the basis of Freud" (*HB*, 343).

The nobility of naturalness can be seen in the classical moral virtues such as courage and magnanimity, virtues cultivated by habit and the development of strength of character which rises above the ordinary, especially in the tragedies of classical literature. The nobility of unnaturalness, on the other hand, is seen in the "integrity" of O'Connor's characters in their struggles with the single-minded pursuit of Christ. The violence which O'Connor brings out in her stories is what might be called the violence of integrity. Integrity, she says, is often a matter of what we cannot do. Hazel Motes, for example, cannot deny Christ although he very much wants to deny him. In the writer who is a prophet we see this same violence. The prophetic writer is called to "intrude upon the timeless ... by the violence of a single-minded respect for truth" (*MM*, 83). The violence of this intense desire for truth appears as a kind of ruthlessness, bringing us to the very edge of evil, getting to the bottom of the meaning of original sin.

"Our age not only does not have a very sharp eye for the almost imperceptible intrusions of grace, it no longer has much feeling for the nature of the violences which precede and follow them" (*MM*, 112). The writer wants to bring out these almost imperceptible intrusions of grace, but "the lines of motion" that he must trace are usually invisible for "they are lines of spiritual motion" (*MM*, 113). The writer wants to capture that moment in which the character changes. This is an invisible change that has to be made visible so that the possibility of such a change in this particular character is believable. Since the action of grace itself is impossible to see, the violences which precede and follow it allow us to notice the struggle within the character, the struggle of free will. O'Connor says that "free will does not mean one will, but many wills conflicting in one man. Freedom cannot be conceived simply. It is a mystery and one which a novel, even a comic novel, can only be asked to deepen" (*WB*, 1).

In "A Good Man is Hard to Find," the violence that precedes the moment of grace is out of sight, indicated only by the sound of gunshots as the Grandmother's family is murdered. As The Misfit confronts his own condition, his voice begins to crack, and the Grandmother suddenly reaches out to him in a moment of unselfishness. The reaction of The Misfit, as he shoots her three times in the chest, is a shocking, sudden indication that something of the greatest significance has just occurred. The Grandmother has accepted the grace that had been offered through The Misfit's cracking voice, while The Misfit rejects—three times—the grace that is offered to him through her touch.

O'Connor says that in her stories there is a moment in which there is an indication that grace has been offered and is either accepted or rejected. "All my stories are about the action of grace on a character who is not very willing to support it" (*HB*, 275). In fact, in most cases, grace is rejected (*HB*, 373). The possibility of the rejection of grace shows that the moment of grace is, at the same time, the moment of freedom.[16]

---

16 Pascal's views on grace and freedom are, of course, complex and the subject of much controversy. However, in the eighteenth Provincial letter, he

O'Connor's use of violence suggests something of the place of the psychic realities in the Christian life. Pascal shows us what this struggle is and why it is painful: "Our Lord said that since the coming of John the Baptist, that is to say since His own advent in the world, and consequently since His advent in all the faithful, the Kingdom of God has been suffering violence, and that the violent take it by force." The two "opposing forces" of our attachment to ourselves and the action of God drawing us to himself are the cause of this violence. "We are unaware of a bond when we voluntarily follow him who leads us on, as St. Augustine says. But when we begin to resist and to withdraw, we suffer greatly; the bond is stretched and undergoes heavy strain, and this strain is our own body which is broken only in death." Indeed, "we must resolve to suffer this warfare all our life, for there is no peace here below. Jesus Christ came to send not peace but a sword" (*SW*, 144–45).

To the young man who is struggling with his hesitation to become a Catholic, O'Connor says that she hopes he can find the experience he needs to make the leap to Christianity, and she recommends Pascal to him. Ultimately, the experience which O'Connor wants to create for such a reader is the possibility of "an encounter with the God of Abraham, Isaac, and Jacob" (*MM*, 161). Pascal's own such experience recorded in a fragment

---

defends the Jansenists against the Jesuits who accuse them of the heresy of Calvin. The Jansenists, he argues, hold to the notion of "efficacious grace," the doctrine propounded by St. Augustine and St. Thomas. The Jansenists "know only too well that man, of his very nature, always has the power to sin and to resist grace, and that since his corruption he bears within him an unfortunate residue of concupiscence which enormously increases this power; but yet that, when it pleases God to touch man by his mercy, he makes him to do what he wants and in the way he wants. Yet this infallibility of God's operation in no way impairs man's natural liberty." (*PL*, 282) There is no contradiction between the sovereign power of grace over free will and the ability of free will to resist grace. O'Connor does not enter into this theological debate, but she does clearly affirm that the acceptance or rejection of grace is a free act.

entitled "The Memorial." On the night of November 23, 1654 for about two hours, Pascal experienced the "fire" of the "'God of Abraham, God of Isaac, God of Jacob,' not of philosophers and scholars" (*P*, #913). Of her own life, O'Connor says that all of her own experience has been that of one "who believes, again in Pascal's words, in the 'God of Abraham, Isaac, and Jacob and not of the philosophers and scholars.'" (*MM*, 161). It is the God of Abraham, Isaac, and Jacob whom she finds when she looks through the common, familiar, and ordinary to the mystery of redemption. In this encounter, the historical embodied reality of the incarnation is recovered for the modern mind.

6. Conversion: From Modern Consciousness to Christian Consciousness

O'Connor tells us that a story is a complete dramatic action and that, in a complete story, the action fully illuminates the meaning of the story. The meaning of her stories is always centered on the possibility of Christian conversion, and the possibility of conversion is always a mysterious interweaving of divine and human action, an interweaving of the offering of divine grace and the acceptance or rejection of the grace that is offered.

In every age, man is in the state of original sin and in need of redemption. Constant conversion, therefore, is always necessary for the Christian life and, "where this is absent, we have a pseudo-Christianity which leaves life's real substance untouched."[1] What, then, is the experience of conversion for the modern man? Christian conversion for the modern individual is the recovery of the historical embodied reality of the incarnation from the distortions of spiritualization. It is accomplished

---

1   Guardini, *Modern World*, 159.

through the radical transformation of the human being in the shifting of the center of consciousness from the self to Christ.

For O'Connor, the confrontation and struggle between faith and modern consciousness is a confrontation and struggle, first and foremost, within herself. "When I ask myself how I know I believe, I have no satisfactory answer at all, no assurance at all, no feeling at all. I can only say with Peter, Lord I believe, help my unbelief" (*HB*, 92). She describes this prayer as "the most natural and most human and most agonizing prayer in the gospels" and she thinks this is "the foundation prayer of faith" (*HB*, 476).[2]

O'Connor sees herself in this torment of doubt: "I think there is no suffering greater than what is caused by the doubts of those who want to believe. I know what torment this is, but I can only see it, in myself anyway, as the process by which faith is deepened. A faith that just accepts is a child's faith and all right for children, but eventually you have to grow religiously.... I suffer this way myself" (*HB*, 353–54). The struggle between belief and unbelief is inevitable, for faith is always a "walking in darkness" (*MM*, 184).

O'Connor refers explicitly to Pascal's most fundamental description of Christian conversion: "Pascal wrote in his notebook, 'If I had not known you, I would not have found you'" (*MM*, 160).[3] It is here, then, that we can discern the path of faith available to modern consciousness, the circular path of discovering what was always already there. In the words of the redeemer: "Take comfort: You would not seek me if you had not found me" (*P*, #919) and "You would not seek me if you did not possess me" (*P*, #929). Pascal assures those who seek that Christ "shall be recognized by those who genuinely seek him" (*P*, #427).

---

   2   See Lorraine V. Murray, *The Abbess of Andalusia: Flannery O'Connor's Spiritual Journey* (Charlotte, NC: Saint Benedict Press, 2009), 57–63.

   3   O'Connor is quoting from memory here and her quotation is not precise. The actual fragments from the *Pensées* are #919 and #929.

Belief is first in the heart, in the felt-knowledge which is pre-reflective. Christ is already possessed in the instincts, in the wise blood, of Hazel Motes and young Tarwater. Both resist the full meaning of this possession and try to escape the demand on the self to leave everything and follow Christ. The circularity of conversion consists in the struggle with unbelief and the ultimate return to and embrace of the instinct that was always already there. Conversion is experienced as coming to know more fully what one already knows and knew all along, as deepening the faith that was already present in the heart.

O'Connor's stories, essays, and letters can serve as a roadmap for the path of constant conversion which is necessary for the Christian life as it is experienced in the modern world. I will set out three aspects of Christian conversion in the modern world, as they are presented in O'Connor's works and illuminated by Pascal's philosophy: self-hatred and self-annihilation, the transcendence of the psychological, and the shifting of the center of consciousness from the self to Christ.

First, the experience of conversion begins in the self-hatred which leads to self-annihilation. In the case of Hazel Motes, we can trace out the path of conversion in terms of Pascal's admonition to the searching heart: "You would not seek me if you did not possess me." The tradition is present in Haze in the form of instinct, in "the nameless unplaced guilt" that he feels. He struggles mightily against this instinct, denying the need for redemption. His self-hatred begins in this nameless unplaced guilt. At the beginning of the novel, he declares "I am clean." He is repulsed by the blood of Christ: his "new jesus" will not "foul" his new church with his redeeming blood, for there is no need for redemption. At the end of the novel, Haze acknowledges: "I am not clean." What has happened to transform him is his confrontation with the spiritualization of the incarnation in the form of Onnie Jay Holy's "idea" of Jesus. The idea is man without original sin and thus a jesus who does not shed his blood. Haze comes to recognize the divinity of the God who does shed his blood for our redemption. His declaration that he is not clean is the hatred of self that is necessary in order to finally see the divinity of the crucified Christ. Haze lives out the meaning of Christ's words in the Gospel: "He who loves his life will lose it, and he who hates his life in this world will keep it for eternal life" (John 12:25–26).

As we have seen, in his confrontation with Montaigne's reduction of the tradition to mere custom, Pascal penetrates to the core of the tradition, showing the uniqueness of Christianity among all other religions. The core of the tradition demands the assent of the searching heart. "No other religion has proposed that we should hate ourselves. No other religion therefore can please those who hate themselves and seek a being who is worthy of love. And if they had never [before] heard of the religion of a humiliated God, they would at once embrace it" (P, #220).

Those who hate themselves see that the religion of a humiliated God *must be* true. It is the only religion that *could be* true. Only the mystery of the ignominious death of Christ can make sense of the journey of the searching mind: the path of the deepening of faith ends at the foot of the cross. When all is said and done, "what makes them believe is the Cross" (P, #842). There, the searching heart recognizes that *this* is what it has been looking for. Here, Christ is *recognized* by those who seek him.

Pascal says that God is more hidden in the incarnation than in nature. In Christ, he remains among other men with no outward difference. Indeed, in his passion, he looks no different from the lowliest human being: scorned, abandoned, and reviled. It takes the eyes of the heart, the eyes of faith, to discern the divinity in such lowliness. Only those who have come to hate themselves can see this. By identifying the core of the tradition as belief in the humiliated God, Pascal shows that this belief is the great *obstacle* for the searching modern mind. Faith is to know "who God really is: not the 'absolute' but—let us dare the word—the 'human' God. Precisely here lies our chief difficulty, in his humanity. God cannot be so! we protest. His flesh and blood is simultaneously revelation and veil. The tangible erects walls: that which makes revelation what it is also shapes our 'stumbling block'."[4]

Conversion is a turning away from oneself to Christ, and this turning is such a radical and complete rejection and denial of the self that it must be described in the extreme terms of hatred of oneself. The self must be hated because it is hateful, and it is hateful on account of its self-love. Pascal says: "The self is hateful" for "the self make[s] itself the center of everything" (P, #597). Further, "all men naturally hate each other" (P, #210). The self, then, has two characteristics: "It is unjust in itself for making itself the center of everything" and "each self is the enemy of all the others and would like to tyrannize them" (P, #597).

Romano Guardini claims that, for Pascal, the most important statement about the human personality is that "the self is hateful."[5] The self comes to recognize itself as hateful only in the recognition of its sinfulness. "The essence of sin is selfishness, the will to not depend on God, but to exist in oneself. Man loves himself; he makes himself and his world the center of existence."[6] For "sin is self-love, pride, the pretension of the self to be the center of existence…. Thus only the heart 'which really hates itself' is capable of this inner purification, of this *reversal of the orientation of existence*, of this fundamental transformation, which is necessary."[7]

Hatred of oneself requires a kind of detachment from oneself which is so great that it overcomes the strongest natural love of oneself. Romano Guardini explains the fundamental difference between the "dangerous detachment" of the mind in Montaigne's philosophical reflection and the detachment from self required for Pascal's hatred of self. Montaigne's detachment is his own act of liberation from his natural self in order to become sufficient unto himself, while Pascal's detachment is "that distance

---

4   Guardini, *The Lord*, 297.
5   Guardini, *Pascal*, 110–11.
6   Guardini, 116.
7   Guardini, 119–20, emphasis added.

from oneself, that view of oneself, that detachment from oneself, which bring about … salutary hate of self and love of God. But this is grace, and God alone can give it."[8]

Pascal writes that "true conversion consists in self-annihilation" (P, #378). As Paul Griffiths puts it: "Our sense of ourselves must be burned to the ground, and that is not something we can do by or to ourselves."[9] This experience of being burned to the ground is, as Michael Moriarty describes it, an experience of humiliation: "When our individual will is thwarted, our self-love wounded, and our ordinary complacent relationship with ourselves shattered, we are most open to the irruption of God's otherness—that is, to grace."[10]

The meaning of Christian conversion, beginning (as it must) in self-hatred, brings out more clearly the very radical nature of Pascal's critique of modern self-consciousness. He sees through this philosophical self-consciousness to its hidden self-deception, to its source in rebellion against the power of God and the givenness of Creation, that is, its source in original sin. When Pascal looks at the human being brought into existence in the act of self-consciousness, he sees neither the pure and transparent mind of the objective observer nor the innocent passive subject. Rather, he sees the hateful self which wants to make itself the center of everything. Conversion demands, then, the recognition of the original sin of pride, and in particular, the pride of intellect which O'Connor presents in the characters of Hazel, Hulga, and Rayber. Conversion requires repentance and humility, for the individual must recognize his need for redemption and forgiveness.

---

8 Guardini, 120.
9 Griffiths, *Why Read Pascal?*, 113.
10 Michael Moriarty, "Grace and Religious Belief in Pascal," in *Cambridge Companion to Pascal*, ed. Nicholas Hammond (Cambridge: Cambridge University Press, 2003), 157.

The divinity of Christ is manifested in the forgiveness of sins. In the story of the cure of the paralytic, Christ first says to the man: "Your sins are forgiven." The scribes are shocked by this and accuse Christ of blasphemy because they know that the claim to have power to forgive sins is the claim to be God. Christ then cures the paralysis of the man to prove that "the Son of Man has authority on earth to forgive sins" (Matthew 9: 2–8). Conversion, then, begins in that hatred of oneself which makes it possible to see the divinity of Christ in his power to forgive sins.

Second, conversion in the modern world entails the transcendence of the limits of the psychological. O'Connor insists that one of the greatest obstacles to conversion in the modern world is the pervasiveness of the conviction that human being can be explained entirely by the science of psychology. To the modern mind, self-hatred has to look like a psychological sickness to be cured by a few years of psychoanalysis. Haze's extreme penitential practices would have to be seen as symptoms of a deep psychological problem caused by his grandfather, the crazy, fanatical, waspish prophet whose preaching about sin is stuck in Haze's head like a stinger. But O'Connor sees through the psychological prejudice to the mystery of original sin. Self-hatred is not ultimately a psychological condition, although it may be accompanied by feelings of guilt, shame, and humiliation. If Haze is to be saved, he must come to realize that Jesus is the redeemer who sheds his blood in atonement for Haze's sins.

O'Connor herself experienced the temptation to reduce religious feeling to the merely psychological. In her prayer journal, she struggles with the "mental pain" of dealing with the challenges to the reality of faith which are constantly posed by the psychological explanations of those around her. Indeed, she says that she is always on the brink of assenting to the idea that she is deluding herself and that her faith is due to cowardice (*PJ*, 4, 15–16).

It is helpful, then, to contrast Christian conversion with the change brought about in the individual in the process of psychoanalysis, for psychoanalysis claims to replace the believer's faith in the historical reality of redemption. Jung describes the effects of psychoanalysis which occur as the patient frees himself from the past, from the tradition, and becomes intensely self-conscious: this is a "centering process" in which the "center of gravity of the personality" shifts and he achieves a "new center of equilibrium." The patient becomes centered on himself, wrapped up in his own purpose of bringing the psychic realities within him under the power of consciousness. Through the direction of the psychoanalyst, he becomes "creatively independent" as he experiments with his own nature. This state of fluidity, change, and growth is the height of psychoanalytic conversion.

Victor White notes the remarkable similarities between this psychoanalytic conversion and Christian conversion in "the manner of the integrating of the redemptive process itself as it is observed to take place in an analysis conducted along Jungian lines."[11] Here we see how central the spiritualization of the incarnation is to the attainment of self-consciousness, for the integration of the *idea* of redemption is necessary for the success of this process.

White explains that "although psychological analysis cannot demand contrition of the patient, it is seldom successful unless it brings about something which, at the very least, is not unlike it: a radical change of the patient's conscious outlook, a *metanoia* or change of mind, and with it of his moral valuations and behaviour.... The very enlargement of his consciousness automatically involves a shifting of his whole center of awareness, and with it of his standard of values." White claims that numerous case histories show striking resemblances between the results of analysis and those of religious and moral conversions and in the symbols which emerge from unconscious sources to effect this transformation.[12] However, in spite of the similarities, psychoanalytic conversion and Christian conversion are fundamentally different.

---

[11] White, *God and the Unconscious*, 79.
[12] White, 187.

O'Connor believes that psychoanalysis can, in some cases, be helpful for the believer, but holiness cannot be identified with psychic health. "I admire [Jung] ... the only way that I think he can be used, which is in helping the person face his own psychic realities, or those realities that the great mystics have always faced and that the Church teaches (in spite of Jung's constant contention that she does not) we must face." Facing one's psychic realities may be good medicine but "the real religious person will accept the God of Abraham, Isaac, and Jacob, but not one who is no more than psychic energy. The kind of 'belief' that Jung offers the modern, sick, unbelieving world is simply belief in the psychic realities that are good for it" (*HB*, 382).

In the psychoanalytic process of attaining self-consciousness, the human being gives up his old natural self in order to become the new self-creating individual. He becomes more and more self-centered and self-contained, as we see in Montaigne who "explicitly seeks to make himself the center of his own world."[13] In recovering the reality of the incarnation, on the contrary, the human being gives up his own self and becomes centered on Christ. As Pascal says, man wants to make himself his own center, for the self makes itself the center of everything. But "Jesus Christ is the object of all things, the center toward which all things tend" (*P*, #449).

In turning away from ourselves to Christ, we must, as O'Connor says, face our own psychic realities, the realities which the great mystics face and which the church teaches us we must face. But the way the psychic realities are faced in the process of psychoanalysis and the way they are faced on the path to the cross are very different. For the modern man in search of self-consciousness, the religious impulses and desires must be "spiritualized." That is, they are approached not as pointing to a reality beyond the self which alone can make us whole, but as a means to rise above the

---

13   Storey and Storey, *Why We Are Restless*, 70.

merely biological instincts and make ourselves whole within ourselves and by our own power. The religious impulses, then, are given a purely human meaning. The goal of self-consciousness requires most of all the subjection of the religious impulses to consciousness in an act of self-redemption.

The meaning of Christian conversion can be seen in the way all kinds of human suffering are confronted, contrasted with the way these sufferings are confronted in psychoanalysis. In this we can see how the psychologizing of all aspects of human life is an incomplete and therefore a distorted view of existence. In *The Gift of Self*, Heather Ward addresses the modern notion that holiness is the same as psychological wholeness. "'Wholeness', in this context, generally applies to psychological and emotional well-being and maturity, to the eradication of our personality disorders, to the healing-over of our psychological wounds. In such an approach 'humanity' is totally identified with psycho-physical being, with ego."[14] But, she argues, by identifying holiness with psychological health, "we are actually binding ourselves to the limits of our psycho-physical nature."[15] Our real need, however, is to seek "singleness of intention upon God."[16] This singleness of intention is a kind of self-forgetfulness, losing oneself in the mystery of Jesus Christ.[17] The painful psychic impulses, instincts, and feelings are not necessarily overcome in the change effected by grace. Depression, fear, anxiety, shame may remain, but they are now seen in a different light, for the vision is focused not on the self but on Christ. Grace is experienced in facing our own psychic realities. The shifting of the center of consciousness is worked out concretely in the interaction between the psychic realities of one's particularity and openness to the action of grace.

---

14   Heather Ward, *The Gift of Self* (London: Darton, Longman and Todd, 1990), 68–69.
15   Ward, 81.
16   Ward, 70.
17   Ward, 78.

Baron von Hügel shows us the meaning of Christian consciousness as the view of human life which is large enough to take all of human suffering into itself. Only with Christ "there is the union of the clearest, keenest sense of all the mysterious depth and breadth and length and height of human sadness, suffering, and sin, *and*, in spite of this and through this and at the end of this, a note of conquest and of triumphant joy." This union "is achieved not by some artificial, facile juxtaposition: but the soul is allowed to sob itself out; and *all this its pain gets fully faced and willed, gets taken up into conscious life. Suffering thus becomes the highest form of action*, a divinely potent means of satisfaction, recovery, and enlargement for the soul,—the soul with its mysteriously great consciousness of pettiness and sin, and its immense capacity for joy in self-donation."[18]

To understand the interaction of the psychic realities with grace, we recall O'Connor's insistence that before grace heals, it cuts with the sword that Christ came to bring. Pascal explains why we must suffer this pain. In the shifting of the center from the self to Christ, we experience the two opposing forces of our attachment to ourselves and the action of God drawing us to himself. And so we suffer the pain of recognizing our own sinfulness, our spiritual poverty, and the destruction of our illusions about our own innocence and self-worth.[19]

---

18 Von Hügel, *The Mystical Element*, 27, Emphasis added.

19 The sword which Christ came to bring, which cuts before it heals, can be experienced not only in painful psychic events but also in physical sickness. Both Pascal and O'Connor suffered greatly in this way. In his prayer concerning his illness, Pascal praises God for using this suffering "to destroy all these vain idols" which are the objects of the passions. Indeed, he thanks God for his compassion in "destroying for my sake all things in the feebleness to which Thou hast reduced me." These "deceptive idols" must be annihilated in order to make it possible for Pascal to delight only in God. He implores God's mercy "for the conversion of my heart," a work "that surpasses all the efforts of nature" (SW, 221–22). Although O'Connor reveals little about the acceptance of her physical suffering, it is clear from her letters that her attitude is similar to Pascal's. "I have never been anywhere but sick.

In the transcendence of the limits of the psychological, the individual begins to break free of the closed circle of self-consciousness. In "A Good Man Is Hard to Find," the Grandmother, in the very moment of her greatest fear and concern for herself, when her own life is at stake, forgets her own self to reach out to The Misfit in his distress. It is in this moment that O'Connor allows us to see the offering of grace.

Third, conversion in the modern world is the shifting of the center of consciousness from the self to Christ. When the self gives itself up as the center of existence, when it yields to the call of grace, something totally unexpected happens to it. As Romano Guardini puts it: "For the first time appears the genuine center ... the real self."[20] The genuine center is Christ.

Baron von Hügel explains how this radical change is the interweaving of divine and human action: "The more costly is our act of love or of sacrifice, ... and the more truly it is our own deepest self-expression, so much the more, at the same time, is this action a thing received as well as given, and that we have it to give, and that we can and do give it, is itself a pure gift of God.... Grace and the Will thus rise and fall, in their degree of action, together; and man will never be so fully and intensely himself, as when he is most possessed by God."[21]

The self-forgetfulness of O'Connor's stance as a writer is her own living out of the self-abandonment to which all Christians are called. In a letter to a friend who questions the meaning of self-abandonment, she writes: "You confuse self-abandonment in the Christian sense with a refusal to be yourself, with self-torture, and suggest that it implies a scorn of God.... Writing is a good example of self-abandonment. I never completely forget

---

In a sense, sickness is a place, more instructive than a long trip to Europe, and it's always a place where there's no company, where nobody can follow. Sickness before death is a very appropriate thing and I think those who don't have it miss one of God's mercies" (HB, 163).

20 Guardini, *Pascal*, 136.
21 Von Hügel, *The Mystical Element*, 80.

myself except when I am writing and I am never more completely myself than when I am writing. It is the same with Christian self-abandonment. The great difference between Christianity and the Eastern religions is the Christian insistence on the fulfillment of the individual person" (*HB*, 457–58).

The experience of the shifting of the center from the self to Christ is the "deepening of conversion" which O'Connor describes as "continually turning inward toward God and away from your own egocentricity" (*HB*, 430). The self, the ego, becomes unimportant. Now, when the individual turns "inward," he finds Christ, not himself.

The transformation effected in Christian conversion begins in hatred of self and ends in love of the being who is "within" us. Pascal writes: "The true and only virtue is therefore to hate ourselves ... and to seek for a being really worthy of love in order to love him. But as we cannot love what is outside us, we must love a being who is within us but is not our own self.... The kingdom of God is within us, and is both ourselves and not ourselves" (*P*, #564).

But what does Pascal mean when he says that Christ is "within" us? What does O'Connor mean when she describes conversion as "constantly turning inward toward God"? Is "within" simply a spatial metaphor to suggest some vaguely apprehended spiritual meaning? Is the claim that Christ is our true self merely a way of expressing the "inner transcendence" of Gnostic spiritualization?

I believe that we can at least begin to grasp what it means to say that Christ is within us by appealing to O'Connor's understanding of anagogical signification. 'Within' is not a mere metaphor. It signifies the reality of our participation in the divine life through grace. Christ is "both ourselves and not ourselves" because we share in his divine life. The reality of that participation is captured in the change that takes place in the moment of grace and in the re-orientation of the whole person to Christ.

In his *Manual for Interior Souls*, Father Jean Grou explains that when the soul has died to itself, has died to self-love, what happens is "more than union; it is transformation; it is *oneness*.... God will pass into his creature, and the creature will pass into God; they shall have one same Life, and one same principle of life."[22] In the saint "Christ has become identified with the essential self of the man, so that the Pauline text: 'It is no longer I who live, but Christ who lives in me,' can be completed by another: 'and now for the first time I really am becoming my true self'."[23]

How is the shifting of the center of consciousness to Christ experienced in the life of the believer? In her stories, letters, and essays, O'Connor leads us more deeply into the meaning of conversion. She displays and illuminates the experience of the mystery of grace, shows the effects of grace in the deepening of faith, and clarifies the meaning of Christian charity.

Conversion is always an interweaving of divine and human action. The action of O'Connor's stories is always captured in the moment of grace in which a decision must be made in the individual's free response to the offering of grace, the moment of the possibility of real change at the deepest level of the personality. The mystery of the action of conversion, as it is made visible in Hazel Motes and young Tarwater, is manifested first in the fact that both are reluctant prophets. They become what they do not want to be. The progress of conversion in their lives is worked out in the struggle within themselves. We might say that "consciously" they resist the pull of Christ toward himself. But deep within them is the instinct, the wise blood, inherited from a crazy backwoods prophet. In this struggle between mind and instinct, between consciousness and the unconscious, the mystery of conversion is played out in O'Connor's stories.

---

[22] John Grou, SJ, *Manual for Interior Souls: A Collection of Unpublished Writings*, trans. Victor Lecoffre (Paris: Christ the King Library, n.d.), 55.

[23] Romano Guardini, *The Humanity of Christ: Contributions to a Psychology of Jesus*, trans. Ronald Walls (Providence, RI: Cluny Media, 2018), 10. Citing Galatians 2:20.

The mystery of conversion is revealed in the fact that the experience of grace is not an experience of grace itself, for we are not "conscious" of grace itself. The action of grace changes a character, and the effect of grace can only be experienced and seen in the change. In a letter to a Protestant friend who was about to enter the church, O'Connor tells him something of her own experience as a Catholic. "Having been a Protestant, you may have the feeling that you must feel you believe; perhaps feeling belief is not always an illusion but I imagine it is most of the time" (*HB*, 164). Although the experience of conversion is the experience of a change in oneself, it is not an experience of a "spiritual" feeling.

In her description of the action of grace, O'Connor says that grace works through nature but entirely transcends nature so that the soul is always open to possibility and the unexpected. The transformation effected by grace is a transformation of the heart, of the will, not of the feelings. In the Wager, Pascal advises those who want to believe not to study the philosophers but to act as though they believe. This subdues their passions and, without understanding how, they begin to believe. In the same spirit, O'Connor refers to a letter written by Gerard Manley Hopkins to a friend who had asked him how he could possibly come to believe, probably expecting a metaphysical answer. But Hopkins only said, "Give alms" (*HB*, 164).

The mystery of conversion is experienced in the fact that we do not have the assurance of feeling the presence of grace, for the change effected by conversion can only be realized and recognized in one's actions. We do not have the certitude of feeling. O'Connor explains that she is "just trying to isolate this kind of abandonment of self which is the result of sanctifying grace." (*HB*, 455). Feelings of certitude about the strength of our faith are not reliable, for faith is not the same as psychic certitude and cannot depend on feelings of certitude. "About the only way we know whether we believe or not is by what we do" (*HB*, 476).

The change effected in the actions of the believer is always a turning away from oneself toward others. Conversion is the reversal of the orientation of existence and, in this reversal, what is demanded of the heart is the love, the Christian charity, which does not and cannot spring from human sources alone. "It is a new level of action and existence which cannot be attained from the natural order, and above all not from the natural order tainted by sin."[24] The relationship with the God of Abraham, Isaac, and Jacob recognized through faith is the experience of an encounter which affects every action of the believer. This, O'Connor says, is "Pascal's experience after his conversion" (*MM*, 160).

O'Connor identifies this charity as an action, not a feeling: "the kind of concern [for others] I mean is a doing, not a feeling" (*HB*, 455) for "you will have found Christ [only] when you are concerned with other people's sufferings and not your own" (*HB*, 453). The shifting of the center from the self to Christ extends necessarily to the individual's relationship to others: "God is to be experienced in Charity (in the sense of love for the divine image in human beings)" (*HB*, 476). Christian conversion begins in the hatred of self which annihilates the self that makes itself the center, hates all other men, and wants to dominate them; it ends in love for Christ and for the image of Christ in human beings.

The experience of conversion, then, is very different from the psychotherapeutic experience of bringing the unconscious pushes and pulls under the power of consciousness and becoming what one wants to be. Conversion is worked out in facing the psychic forces within us and bringing them under the directedness of the will to Christ, not under the directedness of the will to oneself. In Christian conversion, the agent is not transformed into what he wants to be, for the change that occurs in him is not anything he could know in advance. He acts on trust in something beyond himself, allowing grace to change him. O'Connor shows us what it means to live in the presence of this mystery of grace and to live in the attitude of openness to the offering of grace.

---

24   Guardini, *Pascal*, 119–20.

In the absence of any psychological assurances, it is only faith that makes it possible for the human being to trust, to walk out on the water. Faith, for the modern mind, requires the love of truth which Pascal identifies as "the greatest of Christian virtues" (*P*, #979). This is a striking claim: that love of truth is a specifically *Christian* virtue and that it is the *greatest* Christian virtue. Why would Pascal make this claim at the beginning of the modern world? Why does the modern world need to know this? Pascal's own project, as I have presented it, is his revision of the medieval formula of "faith seeking understanding" to "understanding seeking faith." The love of truth leads the modern individual back to the truth of revelation and the truth of the tradition.

In the character of Hulga, O'Connor is presenting us with the outcome of modern philosophy, for modern philosophy has replaced the pursuit of truth with the pursuit of power. Hulga's nihilism is the denial of the possibility of truth. She sees through everything to nothingness and meaninglessness because, for her, everything is a matter of the mind's control. In the character of Hazel Motes, on the contrary, integrity is grounded in the love of truth. When Sabbath Lily screams at him: "You didn't want nothing but Jesus!" Haze answers: "I don't want nothing but the truth!" All along, through all of his denials, Haze is actually driven by the greatest Christian virtue. Love of truth ultimately means submission to the truth of revelation, a humble submission which overcomes precisely the pride of intellect of modern man in rejecting the tradition: "Belief in a divine Revelation seems to involve something like a repentance in the sphere of the intellect."[25] Humility and love of truth are inseparable virtues, united in overcoming the pride of intellect which is the hallmark of modernity.

The action of conversion finds its clearest expression in Christian charity. The practice of Christian charity in the modern world requires

---

25 Michael B. Foster, *Mystery and Philosophy* (London: SCM Press, 1957), 28.

the virtue of humility in a way that responds to the modern contempt for Christian humility. For Romano Guardini, the decisive characteristic of the Christian message of salvation "is expressed in a word which in the course of the modern age has lost its meaning: humility." Humility has become synonymous with the weakness and cowardice which Nietzsche calls "decadence" and "slave morality."[26] However, "true Christian humility is a virtue of strength, not of weakness." For Christ "emptied himself, taking the form of a servant, being made in the likeness of men, and in habit formed as a man. He humbled himself, becoming obedient unto death, even to the death of the cross" (Philippians 2:6–8).

Pascal gives us insight into what O'Connor means by charity as the Christian re-orientation of existence in his presentation of the three "orders" which define the possible orientations of the human being. He sets out "the carnal order" as the order of wealth and power, "the intellectual order" as the order of the mind, and "the order of the heart" as the order of holiness, charity, and humility. "The heart has its order, the mind has its own, which uses principles and demonstrations. The heart has a different one.... Jesus Christ and St. Paul possess the order of charity, not of the mind, for they wished to humble, not to teach. The same with St. Augustine" (P, #298).

The order of the heart is the highest order because it is the order of the lowliness of Jesus. "Jesus, without wealth or any outward show of knowledge has his own order of holiness. He made no discoveries; he did not reign, but he was humble, patient, thrice holy to God, terrible to devils, and without sin. With what great pomp and marvelously magnificent array he came to the eyes of the heart, which perceive wisdom!" Therefore, "it would have been pointless for Our Lord Jesus Christ to come as a king with splendor in his reign of holiness, but he truly came with splendor in his own order. It is quite absurd to be shocked at the

---

26 Guardini, *Modern World*, 141.

lowliness of Jesus, as if his lowliness was of the same order as the greatness he came to reveal" (P, #308).

In a fragment entitled "The Mystery of Jesus," Pascal takes us further into the mystery of the divine humility of Christ. He chooses the scene of the agony in the garden to bring out as fully as possible this profound mystery. "Jesus suffers in his passion the torments inflicted upon him by men, but in his agony he suffers the torments which he inflicts on himself. *He was troubled.* This punishment is inflicted by no human, but an almighty hand, and only he that is almighty can bear it." Only a divine being could do what Christ did (P, #919).[27]

Guardini explains that "all creaturely humility has its origin in the act in which the Son of God became man." Christ humbles himself out of "pure freedom," not out of any need.[28] What we see in the life of Jesus, his words, actions, and relations with others is, over and over again, "supreme power converted into humility." Christ's free acceptance of "the lowliness of the slave" and "the form of a slave" signifies not weakness but strength.[29]

The centrality of humility for the Christian life in the modern world shows us more clearly the wisdom of Pascal's identification of the core of the Christian tradition as belief in "the humiliated God." Humility is a Christian virtue at all times and in all places. However, the form which pride takes in the sovereign modern self requires this emphasis on descent from the superiority of spiritualization to the recognition of the divinity in this humiliated God.

In Hulga, Rayber, and The Misfit, we encounter the way in which pride manifests itself in the truly modern man. Rayber feels the psychological pull to love his son, but he must regard it as irrational. He cannot make

---

27 See Joseph Ratzinger, *Jesus of Nazareth: Holy Week: From the Entrance into Jerusalem to the Resurrection*, trans. Philip J. Whitmore (San Francisco: Ignatius Press, 2011), 68, 156.

28 Guardini, *Modern World*, 142–43.

29 Guardini, 144–45.

sense of it for he does not regard his son as truly human. The Grandmother recognizes the humanity of The Misfit, and she reaches out to touch him: he is one of her children. The Misfit, on the other hand, does recognize the humanness of the Grandmother, but is horrified by it, and instinctively, he draws back and shoots her. He despises her humanity because he cannot believe that God actually became a man. Both Rayber and The Misfit have fallen over the stumbling block of the incarnation. In the shifting of the center of consciousness to Christ, the believer comes to understand that the recognition of the humanity of even the lowliest human being is inseparable from the love of Christ. The realization of that inseparability in one's actions is the essential manifestation of the Christian consciousness in the modern world.

7. The Misfit's Prophetic Vision and Contemporary Culture

We return now to our initial questions. What does it mean to be Catholic in the modern world? What is the experience of the believer who wants to understand how faith might make sense of the human condition in a culture which is thoroughly secular and increasingly hostile to Christianity, and to Catholic faith in particular?

In *The End of the Modern World*, inspired by his study of Pascal, Romano Guardini writes: "There is only one standard by which any epoch can be fairly judged: in view of it own peculiar circumstances, to what extent did it allow for the development of human dignity?"[1] Guardini gives an account of the path which has led us to our own epoch, to this point where our culture has been purged of almost every vestige of Christian belief.[2]

---

1   Guardini, *Modern World*, 22–23.
2   We do encounter public expressions of religious belief in our culture, but these can only be regarded as the merely private opinions and preferences of individuals or groups of individuals who happen to share the same privately held

The Christian tradition of the Middle Ages had brought together the classical understanding of man within nature and the revealed truth of our fallen nature. Medieval man understood himself as a being within the natural hierarchy. He could account for himself as the "rational animal" who had his natural place between the lower animals and the angels. Medieval culture was the reflection and public expression of this harmony of classical thought and Christian revelation. Guardini concludes that "the medieval achievement was so magnificent [with respect to the standard of human dignity] that it stands with the loftiest moments of human history."[3]

Modern man broke away from the classical-medieval hierarchy in which he found his place in nature, for modern science shows him a natural world in which he cannot be at home. The culture gradually abandoned the hierarchical standards grounded in the nature of the human species in favor of the freedom of the individual. Guardini refers to this new modern understanding of the human being as "personality," the very term which O'Connor uses to express the mystery of human being. Although not fully recognized in medieval thought, the modern notion of "personality" is actually dependent upon Christian revelation, was always present in the Christian understanding of human being, and could not have emerged apart from Christian revelation because it signifies the human being in his personal relationship to God: the individual is a "person" because of his relationship to God, not because of his place within nature. "Personality is essential to man. This truth becomes clear, however, and can be affirmed only under the guidance of Revelation, which related man to a living, personal God."[4] Guardini's account of personality captures the meaning of Pascal's understanding of human being in the modern world.

---

opinions. Christianity is allowed no public moral authority and is very deliberately excluded from public discourse. Further, the institutions which see themselves as forming the culture are, for the most part, hostile to Christianity.

3   Guardini, *Modern World*, 22–23.
4   Guardini, 98.

Thus, in the modern realization of "personality," the core of the Christian tradition was not abandoned but rather preserved without the non-essential historical accretion of the classical-medieval understanding of nature and man's place in nature. That is precisely Pascal's task as a philosopher: to preserve the core of the tradition for modern man in the aftermath of the new science of nature.

However, at the same time that modernity moved away from classical culture, it also moved away from the authority of revelation, regarding submission of the mind to revelation as a kind of enslavement. Human freedom, the freedom of personality guaranteed by revelation, was insufficient: only complete individual "autonomy" would do. Thus, modern man engages in an act of self-deception: he claims that the ethical standard of the inherent worth of every human being at the foundation of modern culture did not come from Christianity but was discovered by man himself in the progress of his history. "Modern man's dishonesty was rooted in his refusal to recognize Christianity's affirmation of the God-man relationship. Even as the modern world acclaimed the worth of personality and of an order of personal values, it did away with their guarantor, Christian Revelation."[5] This fundamental dishonesty is the "hypocrisy which denied Christian doctrine and a Christian order of life even as it usurped its human and cultural effects."[6]

I have argued that modern man's self-deception can be understood as the spiritualization of the incarnation which is manifested in the self-consciousness of Montaigne and Jung, and which O'Connor portrays so forcefully in the characters of Hazel Motes, Hulga, and Rayber. The meaning of the incarnation is abstracted from the historical embodied reality of Christ and placed in the service of human self-sufficiency: man without God is sufficient unto himself and bears his own dignity within himself.

---

5   Guardini, 99.
6   Guardini, 105.

In fact, however, the ethical standard of the dignity of every human person cannot persist "unless the Christian concept of the person is vigorously maintained. As soon as the true value of the person is lost, as soon as the Christian faith in the God-man relationship pales, all related attitudes and values begin to disappear."[7] Without divine revelation, the human being can have no consciousness "of the real person who is the absolute ground of each man, an absolute ground superior to every psychological or cultural advantage or achievement. The knowledge of what it means to be a person is inextricably bound up with the Faith of Christianity. An affirmation and a cultivation of the personal can endure for a time, but gradually they too will be lost."[8]

So, again, we must ask how the Christian life is possible at the end of the modern world. Have we not been placed in an impossible situation, in a culture that has been emptied of all Christian substance? If God has placed us in this historical era, then we must believe that we will be able to live in it as Christians. Guardini insists that regret for the harmonious culture of the Middle Ages is not the proper response of the Catholic at the end of the modern world. Faith tells us that "all we can do is accept the present situation and, strengthened by the purest powers of mind and of grace, overcome [the dangers of our situation] from within."[9]

Gaurdini acknowledges the attraction of the Middle Ages as the ideal situation for the possibility of faith. "Naturally, from a Christian point of view, it is decline when the modern age as a whole draws away from Revelation; and it is understandable that the Christian interpretation of history dwells affectionately on the Middle Ages."[10] However, he warns that the medieval harmonious condition of faith and culture can also tend to conceal the full meaning and reality of our fall and our need for

---

7 Guardini, 99.
8 Guardini, 98–99.
9 Guardini, 161.
10 Guardini, 159.

redemption: "In certain periods, under certain conditions, this fact can be concealed more easily than in others."[11] O'Connor also recognizes the "tendency of Catholics to despise the modern world on principle and to condemn out of hand anything that does not have obvious roots in the Middle Ages." Her Pascalian vision allows her to see "the potential power of the modern world to lead a man closer to God" (*Pres*, 158–59).

While medieval culture lent itself to the concealment of our true condition, that condition can no longer be obscured at the end of the modern world, in the total separation of faith and culture. Guardini foresees that the path of modernity ends in the rejection of even the "humanistic" secularized version of Christianity: "The new age will declare that the secularized facets of Christianity are sentimentalities. This declaration will clear the air.... This danger within the new world will also have its cleansing effect upon the new Christian attitude which in a special way must possess both trust and courage."[12] When the air is cleared, we can see what the moral world looks like when the worth of the individual human being is detached from belief in the incarnation. At that point, we are at the end of the modern world and the true meaning of the self without God emerges. The great gift that is given to us in our present condition is clarity about the meaning of a culture without Christianity.

Guardini insists that it is good that modern dishonesty was unmasked. "As the benefits of Revelation disappear even more from the coming world, man will truly learn what it means to be cut off from Revelation.... The rapid advance of a non-Christian ethos ... will be crucial for the Christian sensibility. As unbelievers deny Revelation more decisively, as they put their denial into more consistent practice, it will become the more evident what it really means to be a Christian."[13]

---

11   Guardini, 161.
12   Guardini, 105.
13   Guardini, 100–101.

What is gained in the loss of all cultural constraints is prophetic vision: to see the moral world as it really is, to have no illusions about the innocence of human power, and no illusions about the true source of all goodness. O'Connor and Pascal see through the common, familiar, and ordinary to the mystery of the incarnation for they see the human world entirely in terms of sin and redemption. They give us a moral landscape devoid of the naturally given standards of the noble and the base, of the honorable and the shameful, and of the classical virtues assimilated by the culture of the Middle Ages. In rejecting the classical-medieval hierarchy, Pascal shows us our essential "displacement." Man is no longer at home in the world: man is a freak on account of original sin.

O'Connor insists that drama "bases itself on the bedrock of original sin, whether the writer thinks in theological terms or not" (*MM*, 167). She takes us down through the darkness of the psychological to the bedrock of original sin and the reality of human nature which shows itself when all cultural restraints have been abandoned and all psychological explanations have been exhausted. That is the stark Pascalian landscape of her stories.

"A Good Man Is Hard to Find" is set perfectly against the background of this landscape. In the character of The Misfit, O'Connor shows us the condition of the human being at the end of the modern world.

It is The Misfit who gives expression to O'Connor's Pascalian vision: "Jesus thrown everything off balance." The Misfit sees through the diagnosis of the psychiatrist to the mystery of original sin. He sees the disproportion between the actions of which he is conscious and the burden of his guilt and responsibility. He knows that his guilt is real. He also recognizes the terrible disproportion between the innocence of Christ and the punishment Christ suffers at the hands of human justice.

Like Pascal, The Misfit sees that faith in the divinity of Christ demands that a choice be made. He knows that the choice is between good and evil, between following Christ and committing murder. "Jesus was the only One that ever raised the dead and he shouldn't have done it. He thrown everything off balance. If He did what He said, then it's nothing for you to do but throw everything away and follow him, and if he didn't, then it's nothing for you to do but enjoy the few minutes you got left the best way you can—by killing somebody or burning down his house or doing some other meanness to him. No pleasure but meanness" (CS, 132).

Pascal's thought moves from the natural moral world in which all men hate each other and want to dominate each other to the truth of the incarnation as the only alternative to the hateful self. The Misfit is separated from all cultural constraints: he has escaped from the law and is in a position to do whatever he wants to the Grandmother and her family. He has complete power over them. The Misfit recognizes the evil of his own condition and knows that, if he believed in the incarnation, he would not be what his is. "If I had of been there I would of known and I wouldn't be like I am now" (CS, 132). That is the clarity of his prophetic vision.

In the choice between Christ and murder, The Misfit offers no third option. There is no possibility of "natural" goodness, no appeal to natural compassion. The incarnation is the only possible alternative to what he has become. Christ is the only source of goodness. In the choice between Christ and murder, The Misfit encounters the meaning of the separation of faith in Christ from recognition of the worth of every human life.

The divorce between human dignity and belief in the presence of Christ in even the lowliest human being is the destruction of human community. In the contemporary world, the weak and lowly are at the mercy of the strong and powerful as never before because Christian attitudes and "values" have disappeared from public life. The sense of superiority of the truly modern man, the enlightened "spiritual" individual who has nothing *human* in common with the "animal" unenlightened masses, manifests itself in contempt for the lowliest human beings. This compartmentalization of mankind encourages an "unbounded arrogance" in those who ascend to true enlightenment.[14] For Jung, the distance between the self-conscious elite and their unselfconscious neighbors could hardly be greater. "Even in our civilization the people who form, psychologically speaking, the lowest stratum, live almost as unconsciously as primitive races" (*MMSS*, 197). The unselfconscious masses of human beings are de-humanized by the elite of truly modern men who rise so far above the animal species as to be a different kind of being.

This division between the enlightened and the unenlightened, which Jung described in the early twentieth century, has become increasingly significant in our social and political life. In the twenty-first century, it is sometimes articulated and defended in the theory of "trans-humanism." Trans-humanism is the belief that humans should strive to transcend the physical limitations of the mind and body by technological means, namely through artificial intelligence. Even if we are inclined to reject the predictions of the trans-humanists as impossible or even preposterous, their claims about the future of mankind reveal the assumptions of these elites concerning the standard of human worth. Like Rayber, the trans-humanists' standard of human worth is usefulness.

Yuval Noah Harari predicts that "the main products of the twenty-first century will be bodies, brains, and minds, and the gap between those who know how to engineer bodies and brains and those who do not will be far bigger than the gap between … [Homo] Sapiens and Neanderthals. In the twenty-first century, those who ride the train of progress will acquire divine abilities of creation and destruction, while those left behind will face extinction."[15] Scientific discoveries and technological developments will "split humankind into a mass of useless humans and a small elite of upgraded superhumans."[16] Harari asks: "As the masses lose their economic

---

14   Von Balthasar, introduction, 1.
15   Yuval Noah Harari, *Homo Deus: A Brief History of Tomorrow* (New York: Harper Collins, 2017), 275.
16   Harari, 355.

importance, will the moral argument alone be enough to protect human rights and liberties? Will elites and governments go on valuing every human being even when it pays no economic dividends?"[17] In Harari's new world, human beings are divided into an elite of "enhanced human beings" who have "divine powers of creation and destruction"[18] and the mass of useless, superfluous, unnecessary people.[19]

Unlike Harari, Jung does recognize the importance of Christianity with respect to the dignity of the individual, especially in the face of the rise of totalitarian forms of government in the modern world. He sees that "in order to turn the individual into a function of the State, his dependence on anything beside the State must be taken from him." However, for Jung, not every man but only the self-conscious individual has the "psychic attitude" which can preserve his freedom (US, 19). The internalized "religious attitude" is the "inner, transcendent experience which alone can protect him from the otherwise inevitable submersion in the mass" (US, 23). Jung claims that "the salvation of the world consists in the salvation of the individual soul" rising up out of the "torpid, mindless mass" (US, 56). Only psychology can bring about "the spiritual transformation of mankind" (US, 108).

But how can there be a society in which such autonomous, isolated individuals live together with the mindless masses? Jung's answer is that society needs a bond of an affective nature, "a principle of a kind like *caritas*, the Christian love of your neighbor" (US, 102). In other words, the superior spiritual elite must unite itself to the inferior masses through an "affective bond" of compassion.

In the contemporary world, Christian charity has been reduced to the sentiment of compassion and compassion has become central to contem-

---

17   Harari, 313.
18   Harari, 47.
19   Harari, 315, 322, 331.

porary discussions of morality. This kind of compassion, however, cannot be the basis for genuine community because it is not a sympathy based on our common humanity, for there is no common humanity. Genuine Christian compassion, on the contrary, must be grounded in our common humanity understood in the terms of original sin and our need for redemption. That is, it is ultimately grounded in the reality of the incarnation.

The co-existence of autonomy and compassion turns out to be impossible to maintain. When compassion is detached from belief in the mystery of salvation, it becomes possible to inflict unspeakable cruelties on the hordes of men and women who cling to the religion of the tradition and who resist the efforts of the elites to re-fashion them in the image of the new man. In her criticism of what she calls "popular pity," O'Connor concludes: "When tenderness is detached from the source of tenderness, its logical outcome is terror. It ends in forced labor camps and in the fumes of the gas chamber" (CW, 830–31).

O'Connor makes it explicit that both Rayber and Hulga do experience a kind of pity. However, Rayber's pity for young Tarwater and Hulga's pity for the Bible salesman are inseparable from their contempt for the unenlightened. Rayber performs "experiments" on both old and young Tarwater. Hulga wants to "experiment" with the supposedly simple Bible salesman. They are interested in the unenlightened only insofar as they can assert power over them and re-create them.

O'Connor is critical of the tendency to the kind of "hazy" compassion and sentimentality so evident in the literary criticism of her day. In her essay on "The Grotesque in Southern Fiction," she says that readers tend to connect the grotesque with the sentimental and associate it with the writer's compassion. "Usually I think what is meant by [compassion] is that the writer excuses all human weakness because human weakness is human.... [but] when the grotesque is used in a legitimate way, the intellectual and moral judgments implicit in it will have the ascendency over feeling" (MM, 43). Her point is that we are all freaks and that we are not to be pitied for undergoing the pain necessary for self-knowledge and conversion. Sentimentality, she says, is "an excess, a distortion of sentiment usually in the direction of an overemphasis on innocence." However, "we lost our innocence in the Fall, and our return to it is through the Redemption which was brought about by Christ's death and by our slow participation in it. Sentimentality is a skipping of this process in its concrete reality and an early arrival at a mock state of innocence" (MM, 147–48).

There is a proper place for compassion, of course, but only when its source is Christ, when it is tied to Christian charity and when suffering is understood within the context of redemption. If Christianity becomes "humanism," if Christian charity is reduced to compassion, then it can no longer be the social bond. Daniel Mahoney, in *The Idol of Our Age: How the Religion of Humanity Subverts Christianity*, writes that the religion of humanity, "woefully ignorant of sin and of the tragic dimension of the human condition, reduces religion to a project of this-worldly amelioration. Free-floating compassion substitutes for charity, and a humanity conscious of its unity (and utter self-sufficiency) puts itself in the place of the visible and invisible Church." If Christianity is redefined in humanitarian terms and shorn of any recognizable transcendental dimension, it becomes nothing more than an instrument for promoting egalitarian social justice.[20] As Mahoney argues, the ethos which results from the reduction of Christian charity to compassion and sympathy is the humanitarian ethos that is easily compatible with fevered support for abortion and euthanasia.[21]

The way in which attitudes toward abortion have changed—from regarding it as a necessary evil to celebrating it as the ultimate manifestation of

---

20   Daniel J. Mahoney, *The Idol of Our Age: How the Religion of Humanity Subverts Christianity* (New York: Encounter Books, 2018), 13.
21   Mahoney, *Idol of Our Age*, 70.

individual autonomy—shows just how easily the co-existence of autonomy and compassion is destroyed. Abortion is a fundamental betrayal of human community for it destroys the sacred bond of mother and child and the generational bond of the living and the unborn. Is it possible to set a firm limit to this de-humanization beyond which we will not go? Recent developments in the wider acceptance of abortion and euthanasia suggest that it is not possible.

O'Connor foresees the justification for abortion, presenting it in her depiction of Rayber's attitude toward his own son, his own flesh and blood. Rayber tells young Tarwater not to pay any attention to Bishop and to pretend he doesn't exist. Indeed, O'Connor has Rayber say about Bishop: "Nothing ever happens to that kind of child. In a hundred years people may have learned enough to put them to sleep when they're born" (*VBA*, 168). Nothing can "happen" to Bishop because he cannot be affected by Rayber's attempts to change him. Bishop will always be "useless." This contempt for the lowest form of human life is echoed in the scene in which Rayber, young Tarwater, and Bishop are eating at a restaurant where some teenagers had gathered. O'Connor describes the way the teenagers looked at Bishop: "Their look was shocked and affronted as if they had been betrayed by a fault in creation, something that should have been corrected before they were allowed to see it" (*VBA*, 190).

As Susan Srigley explains, Rayber "has reduced Bishop's existence to a rationally incomplete, and hence less than fully human, being." For Rayber, "dignity and usefulness reside solely in rational activity."[22] Srigley argues that Bishop expresses "the radical nature of [O'Connor's] vision of spiritual communion."[23] He "anchors the entire novel as the focal point

---

22   Srigley, *Sacramental Art*, 112.
23   Susan Srigley, "Asceticism and Abundance: The Communion of Saints in *The Violent Bear It Away*," in *Dark Faith: New Essays on Flannery O'Connor's* The Violent Bear It Away, ed. Susan Srigley (Notre Dame, IN: University of Notre Dame Press, 2012), 192.

for human responsibility, but more important, for what it means to be a human being."[24] O'Connor's answer to the justification of abortion is simple and direct: "I believe and the Church teaches that God is as present in the idiot boy as in the genius" (*HB*, 99).

While O'Connor rarely discusses politics in her letters and essays, it is clear that she does not believe that political "solutions" are sufficient for establishing a strong social bond. Jerome Foss provides a comprehensive view of O'Connor's works in the context of modern political philosophy. He does not claim that O'Connor offers us a "political philosophy" in the strict sense. Rather, she points beyond politics to an understanding of human being, and in doing so, she shows both the limits of politics and the dangers of governing by compassion.[25]

Foss identifies O'Connor's insights with an Augustinian vision of the "two cities," the city of God and the city of man, pointing out that *The Violent Bear It Away* refers to "the Kingdom of God."[26] He explains that modern political thought is radically different from classical and medieval political thought because it is does not take its bearing from notions of the "common good" or the higher ends of human life. Questions of religious faith are privatized and modernity becomes progressively secular, culminating in the nihilism of Nietzsche.[27] In this situation, it is crucial to recognize and to insist upon the limits of politics, the transcendent character of religion, and the beneficial effects of religion for the social bond. "Religion has salutary political effects and its absence, O'Connor is

---

24 Srigley, *Sacramental Art*, 119. See also, John F. Desmond, "The Lost Childhood of George Rayber," 43. "Rayber's love for Bishop is pure because, given Bishop's handicap, he demands unconditional love, that is, to love him and all creation as it is, absolutely, for its own sake."

25 Jerome C. Foss, *Flannery O'Connor and the Perils of Governing by Tenderness* (Lanham, MD: Lexington Books, 2019), 35.

26 Foss, 59–64.

27 Foss, 79.

convinced, leaves citizens without an adequate compass for exploring the mystery beyond the city."[28]

The church in its bond of charity is the true source of the social bond. Without the presence of the transcendent bond of charity, the realm of politics becomes merely the rule of the strong over the weak, grounded in nothing more than brute force.

At the beginning of the modern age, Pascal embraces a Christian ethic of equality. He admonishes the nobleman: "You must have two ways of looking at things; that if you deal outwardly with men in accordance with your rank you must recognize by a more hidden but more rightful way of thinking that you are not by nature above them. If public opinion raises you above the common run of men, let the other humble you and keep you in perfect equality with all men, for that is your natural station.... Do not delude yourself by believing that your being has something more elevated than that of the others" (SW, 213). This condition of perfect equality can only be founded on Christian charity and cannot be attained through political means. For Pascal, the meaning of Christian community is found in the mystical body of Christ: "*He that is joined to the Lord is one spirit;* we love ourselves because we are members of Christ. We love Christ because he is the body of which we are members. All are one. One is in the other like the three persons [of the Trinity]" (P, #372).

O'Connor's insistence on the Catholic stance of our mutual interdependence reveals her deep sense of human community. Behind her views on the social bond stands the Catholic teaching on tradition, the sacraments, and the mutual interdependence of the members of the church. As Josef Pieper claims: "Real unity among human beings has its roots in nothing else but the common possession of [sacred] tradition."[29] Tradition

---

[28] Foss, 144.
[29] Josef Pieper, *Tradition: Concept and Claim*, trans. E. Christian Kopff (Wilmington, DE: ISI Books, 2008), 68.

implies community, not just the union of those now living but those who have lived in the past and those who will live in the future.

In his "Notes towards the Definition of Culture," T. S. Eliot sets out the conditions for the common culture created by sacred tradition: "While we believe that the same religion may inform a variety of cultures, we may ask whether any culture could come into being, or maintain itself, without a religious basis. We may go further and ask whether what we call the culture, and what we call the religion, of a people are not different aspects of the same thing: the culture being, essentially, the incarnation (so to speak) of the religion of a people."[30] The situation that Eliot describes is one in which "the culture of an artist or a philosopher is distinct from that of a mine worker or a field labourer; the culture of a poet will be somewhat different from that of a politician; but in a healthy society these are all parts of the same culture."[31]

C. S. Lewis, recounting his own experience, gives us a concrete example of what this social bond actually means. He disliked going to church on Sundays; he disliked the hymns which he considered to be fifth-rate poems set to sixth-rate music. "But as I went on I saw the great merit of it. I came up against different people of quite different outlooks and different education, and then gradually my conceit just began peeling off. I realized that the hymns were, nevertheless, being sung with devotion and benefit by an old saint in elastic-side boots in the opposite pew, and *then you realize that you aren't fit to clean those boots*."[32] Natural and conventional differences are not erased, but they become insignificant in the presence of the reality of the incarnation. This transformation is the change of heart to which the believer opens himself and consents.

---

30 T. S. Eliot, *Christianity and Culture: The Idea of a Christian Society and Notes towards the Definition of Culture* (New York: Harcourt, Brace and World, 1949), 101.

31 Eliot, *Christianity and Culture*, 198.

32 C. S. Lewis, *God in the Dock: Essays on Theology and Ethics*, ed. Walter Hooper (Grand Rapids, MI: William B. Eerdmans, 1970), 61–62, emphasis added.

O'Connor writes: "The action by which charity grows invisibly among us, entwining the living and the dead, is called by the Church the Communion of Saints. It is a communion created upon human imperfection, created from what we make of our grotesque state" (*MM*, 228). This communion means that "the burdens we bear because of someone else, we can also bear for someone else" (*HB*, 178). Susan Srigley sees in O'Connor's stories the interdependence which works itself out in the struggle between the idea that human beings are morally interdependent and "the idea that as autonomous individuals, human beings are not responsible for anyone unless they choose to be." This, she says, "is at the heart of O'Connor's ethical fiction."[33] The moment of grace in her stories is the revelation of the interconnectedness of human lives and of love.[34]

In her discussion of *The Violent Bear It Away*, Srigley finds this central theme of "the relation between life and death, or, more precisely, the *relationships* between the living and the dead and the spiritual ties that bind them." O'Connor identifies this ongoing relation with the Christian notion of the communion of saints, which is the heart of a truly spiritual community whose essential interdependence reflects the principle that all human beings are created in the image of God. "This communion is an affirmation of the body and the soul, of the personal and the communal, both as human beings live together in the present, and in the continuing mystery of the connection of lives beyond death."[35]

Christian consciousness is not "solitary" but rather a participation in that mutual interdependence which is essential to the Catholic understanding of the Christian life. O'Connor illustrates this with respect to The Misfit and the Grandmother. Responding to a criticism of her stories, she writes: "You say that there is love between man and God in the stories, but never between people—yet the grandmother is not in the least

---

33   Srigley, *Sacramental Art*, 5.
34   Srigley, 7.
35   Srigley, "Asceticism and Abundance," 186.

concerned with God but reaches out to touch the Misfit" (*HB*, 379). In another letter, she explains how the encounter between the Grandmother and The Misfit manifests her specifically Catholic view of our mutual interdependence. "Grace, to the Catholic way of thinking, can and does use as its medium the imperfect, purely human, and even hypocritical.... The Misfit is touched by the Grace that comes through the old lady when she recognizes him as her child, as she has been touched by the Grace that comes through him in his particular suffering." Although The Misfit shoots her because he is horrified at her humanness, the grace embodied in her touch has worked in him, and he acknowledges that she would have been a good woman if *he* had been there every moment of her life. "In the Protestant view, I think Grace and nature don't have much to do with each other. The old lady, because of her hypocrisy and humanness and banality couldn't be a medium for Grace. In the sense that I see things the other way, I'm a Catholic writer" (*HB*, 389–90).

Grace appears in the inter-action of the Grandmother and The Misfit, embodied in their relationship as mother and child. Their kinship has its roots in the mystery of original sin: The Misfit is a child of Eve. The Grandmother *touches* him. This indestructible interweaving of nature and grace is "the true touchstone of what is Catholic."[36]

The specifically Catholic teaching concerning our mutual interdependence is grounded in the sacrament of the Eucharist, "the central mystery of Christian life."[37] For Pascal, the Eucharist constitutes the community of the church: "The Eucharist, along with the word of Scripture, stood in continuity to the Incarnation of Christ; it was for [Pascal] the last word of Christianity and the most profound expression of the community of the Church."[38] The Eucharist is "the centerpiece of Catholic sacramental life," for "instead of the movement toward God involving progressive

---

[36] Von Balthasar, *The Scandal of the Incarnation*, 53.
[37] Guardini, *The Lord*, 376.
[38] Guardini, *Pascal*, 223–24.

abstraction and repudiation of the order of matter, the movement is toward the concrete and the material." For Pascal, "the presence of the hidden God is nowhere more dramatically at work than in the Eucharist."[39] The Eucharist is the pledge of redemption, for when "the Gnostics tear Christ into two pieces; a mortal man and a spiritual being incapable of suffering; ... they disown the heart of Christianity. Only when matter, Christ's very body, is safeguarded in God, is man redeemed."[40]

Susan Srigley explains how the desire for Christ in the Eucharist enlarges the heart to encompass all men. "Tarwater's desire propels him toward the feast that will truly satisfy *his* hunger, but he arrives to a shared communion: a multitude is gathered with enough food to satisfy *all*," the Eucharistic banquet. This is Tarwater's recognition of human interdependence.[41] "The freedom and autonomy that Tarwater has sought since the death of [Old Tarwater] has come full circle, and he arrives at a place of communion rather than isolation. No longer imposing the free reign of his selfish will, he is himself enlarged by the community that surrounds him. He joins the living and the dead and the feast is *abundant*. He embodies a desire for something larger than himself.... Tarwater learns that this abundance feeds without diminishing, no matter how many are at the feast."[42]

Of her own life, O'Connor says that the Eucharist "is the center of existence for me; all the rest of life is expendable" (*HB*, 125). Truly, the center has shifted from herself to Christ. In "the strangest and most hidden mystery of all," the individual finds transcendence of the limits of his psychic life and participates in the eternal life of Christ. In this lowly humble act of eating, he experiences his embodied humanity. O'Connor's incarnational art is, in her own eyes, her "very minor hymn to the Eucharist."

---

39 Hibbs, *Wagering*, 186–87.
40 Von Balthasar, *The Scandal of the Incarnation*, 53.
41 Srigley, "Asceticism and Abundance," 188.
42 Srigley, 210.

In the incarnation, "the Word was made flesh and dwelt amongst us." As Pascal says: Jesus remained unknown among men with no outward difference, and he remains among us in his lowly, embodied hiddenness, in the strangest and most hidden mystery of all, the Eucharist which hides the redeemer under the appearance of ordinary bread. To see Christ in ordinary men and in ordinary bread is to see with the eyes of faith, to see the most extraordinary in the most familiar.

Bibliography

Aquinas, Thomas. *Summa Theologica*. Translated by Fathers of the English Dominican Province. 5 vols. Notre Dame, IN: Ave Maria, Christian Classics, 1981.

Bacon, Francis. *Novum Organum*. Translated by Peter Urbach and John Gibson. Chicago: Open Court, 1994.

Benichou, Paul. *Man and Ethics: Studies in French Classicism*. Translated by Elizabeth Hughes. Garden City, NY: Doubleday, 1971.

Bosco, Mark, SJ, and Brent Little, eds. *Revelation and Convergence: Flannery O'Connor and the Catholic Intellectual Tradition*. Washington, DC: The Catholic University of America Press, 2017.

Brague, Remi. *The Kingdom of Man: Genesis and Failure of the Modern Project*. Translated by Paul Seaton. Notre Dame, IN: University of Notre Dame Press, 2018.

Candler, Peter M., Jr. "The Anagogical Imagination of Flannery O'Connor." *Christianity and Literature* 60, no. 1 (Autumn 2010): 11–33.

Congar, Yves, OP. *The Meaning of Tradition*. Translated by A. N. Woodrow. San Francisco: Ignatius Press, 2004.

Desmond, John F. "The Lost Childhood of George Rayber." In *Dark Faith: New Essays on Flannery O'Connor's* The Violent Bear It Away, edited by Susan Srigley, 35–56. Notre Dame, IN: University of Notre Dame Press, 2012.

Edmondson, Henry T. *Return to Good and Evil: Flannery O'Connor's Response to Nihilism*. Lanham, MD: Lexington Books, 2002.

———. "'Wingless Chickens': 'Good Country People' and the Seduction of Nihilism." *Flannery O'Connor Review* 2 (2003): 63–73.

Eliot, T. S. *Christianity and Culture: The Idea of a Christian Society and Notes towards the Definition of Culture*. New York: Harcourt, Brace and World, 1949.

———. "The *Pensées* of Pascal." In *Selected Essays*. New York: Harcourt Brace, 1932.

Ference, Damian. *Understanding the Hillbilly Thomist: The Philosophical Foundations of Flannery O'Connor's Narrative Art*. Elk Grove Village, IL: Word on Fire, 2023.

Force, Pierre. "Pascal and Philosophical Method." In *Cambridge Companion to Pascal*, edited by Nicholas Hammond, 216–34. Cambridge: Cambridge University Press, 2003.

Foss, Jerome C. *Flannery O'Connor and the Perils of Governing by Tenderness*. Lanham, MD: Lexington Books, 2019.

Foster, Michael B. *Mystery and Philosophy*. London: SCM Press, 1957.

Fouke, Daniel C. "Pascal's Physics." In *Cambridge Companion to Pascal*, edited by Nicholas Hammond, 75–101. Cambridge: Cambridge University Press, 2003.

Gentry, Marshall Bruce. *Flannery O'Connor's Religion of the Grotesque*. Jackson, MS and London: University Press of Mississippi, 1986.

Gooch, Brad. *Flannery: A Life of Flannery O'Connor*. New York: Little, Brown and Company, 2009.

Griffiths, Paul J. *Why Read Pascal?* Washington, DC: The Catholic University of America Press, 2021.

Grou, John, SJ. *Manual for Interior Souls: A Collection of Unpublished Writings*. Translated by Victor Lecoffre. Paris: Christ the King Library, n.d.

Guardini, Romano. *The Conversion of Augustine*. Translated by Elinor Briefs. Providence, RI: Cluny, 2020.

———. *The End of the Modern World*. Translated by Joseph Theman and Herbert Burke. 1956. Reprint, Wilmington, DE: ISI Books, 1998.

———. *The Humanity of Christ: Contributions to a Psychology of Jesus*. Translated by Ronald Walls. Providence, RI: Cluny Media, 2018.

———. *The Lord*. Translated by Elinor Castendyk Briefs. Washington, DC: Regnery Publishing, 1996.

———. *Pascal for Our Time*. Translated by Brain Thompson. New York: Herder and Herder, 1966. Republished as *Pascal: A Study in Christian Consciousness*. Providence, RI: Cluny Media, 2022.

———. *The World and the Person and Other Writings*. Translated by Stella Lange. Washington, DC: Regnery Gateway, 2023.

Hammond, Nicholas. "Pascal's *Pensées* and the Art of Persuasion." In *Cambridge Companion to Pascal*, edited by Nicholas Hammond, 235–52. Cambridge: Cambridge University Press, 2003.

Harari, Yuval Noah. *Homo Deus: A Brief History of Tomorrow*. New York: Harper Collins, 2017.

Hibbs, Thomas. *Wagering on an Ironic God: Pascal on Faith and Philosophy*. Waco, TX: Baylor University Press, 2017.

Hügel, Baron Friedrich von. *The Mystical Element of Religion as Studied in Saint Catherine of Genoa and Her Friends*. Vol. 1. 2nd ed. New York: E. P. Dutton and Co., 1923.

Ireland, Patrick J. "The Sacred and the Profane: Redefining Flannery O'Connor's Vision." In *Realist of Distances: Flannery O'Connor Revisited*, edited by Karl-Heinz Westarp and Jan Nordby Gretlund, 186–96. Aarhus: Aarhus University Press, 1987.

Irenaeus. *The Scandal of the Incarnation: Irenaeus "Against the Heretics"*. Edited by Hans Urs von Balthasar. Translated by John Saward. San Francisco: Ignatius Press, 1981.

Jones, John. *On Aristotle and Greek Tragedy*. New York: Oxford University Press, 1962.

Jung, Carl Gustav. *Modern Man in Search of a Soul.* Translated by W. S. Dell and Cary F. Baynes. New York: Harcourt, 1933.

———. *The Undiscovered Self.* Translated by R. F. C. Hull. New York: Signet, 2006.

Kinney, Arthur F. *Flannery O'Connor's Library: Resources of Being.* Athens: The University of Georgia Press, 1985.

Kolakowski, Leszek. *God Owes Us Nothing: A Brief Remark on Pascal's Religion and on the Spirit of Jansenism.* Chicago: University of Chicago Press, 1995.

Kruger, Gerhard. "The Origin of Philosophical Self-Consciousness." Translated by Fabrice Paradis Beland. *New Yearbook for Phenomenology and Phenomenological Philosophy* 7 (2007): 209–59. First published in *Logos* 22 (1933): 225–72.

Lake, Christina Bieber. *The Incarnational Art of Flannery O'Connor.* Macon, GA: Mercer University Press, 2005.

Lewis, C. S. *God in the Dock: Essays on Theology and Ethics.* Edited by Walter Hooper. Grand Rapids, MI: Eerdmans, 1970.

Lynch, William F. *Christ and Apollo: The Dimensions of the Literary Imagination.* 1960. Reprinted, Belmont, NC: Wiseblood Books, 2021.

Mahoney, Daniel J. *The Idol of Our Age: How the Religion of Humanity Subverts Christianity.* New York: Encounter Books, 2018.

Malebranche, Nicolas. *Dialogues on Metaphysics and on Religion.* Edited by Nicholas Jolley. Translated by David Scott. Cambridge: Cambridge University Press, 1997.

Manent, Pierre. *Montaigne: Life Without Law.* Translated by Paul Seaton. Notre Dame, IN: Notre Dame University Press, 2020.

McCarthy, John. "Pascal on Certainty and Utility." In *Modern Enlightenment and the Rule of Reason,* edited by John C. McCarthy, 92–123. Washington, DC: The Catholic University of America Press, 1998.

Montaigne, Michel de. *The Complete Essays of Montaigne.* Translated by Donald Frame. Stanford, CA: Stanford University Press, 1943.

Montgomery, Marion. "Flannery O'Connor: Prophetic Prophet." *The Flannery O'Connor Bulletin* 3 (Autumn 1974): 79–95.

———. *The Trouble with You Innerleckchuls*. Front Royal, VA: Christendom College Press, 1988.

———. *Why Flannery O'Connor Stayed Home*. Vol. 1 of *The Prophetic Poet and the Spirit of the Age*. La Salle, IL: Sherwood Sugden and Company, 1981.

Moriarty, Michael. "Grace and Religious Belief in Pascal." In *Cambridge Companion to Pascal*, edited by Nicholas Hammond, 144–61. Cambridge: Cambridge University Press, 2003.

Murray, Lorraine V. *The Abbess of Andalusia: Flannery O'Connor's Spiritual Journey*. Charlotte, NC: Saint Benedict Press, 2009.

Nemoianu, Virgil Martin. "Pascalian Faith and the Place of the Wager." *The Heythrop Journal* 52, no. 1 (2011): 27–39.

O'Connor, Flannery. *The Collected Works*. Edited by Sally Fitzgerald. New York: Library of America, 1988.

———. *The Complete Stories*. New York: Farrar, Straus and Giroux, 1971.

———. *Conversations with Flannery O'Connor*. Edited by Rosemary M. Magee. Jackson, MS and London: University Press of Mississippi, 1987.

———. *The Habit of Being*. Edited by Sally Fitzgerald. New York: Farrar, Straus and Giroux, 1979.

———. *Mystery and Manners*. Edited by Sally and Robert Fitzgerald. New York: Farrar, Straus and Giroux, 1961.

———. *A Prayer Journal*. Edited by W. A. Sessions. New York: Farrar, Straus and Giroux, 2013.

———. *The Presence of Grace and Other Book Reviews*. Compiled by Leo J. Zuber. Edited by Carter W. Martin. Athens: The University of Georgia Press, 1983.

———. *The Violent Bear It Away*. New York: Farrar, Straus and Giroux, 1955.

———. *Wise Blood*. New York: Farrar, Straus and Giroux, 2007.

Pascal, Blaise. *Great Shorter Works*. Translated by Emile Cailliet and John C. Blankenagel. Eugene, OR: Wipf and Stock, 2017.

———. *Pensées*. Translated by A. J. Krailsheimer. London: Penguin Books, 1995.

———. *The Provincial Letters*. Translated by A. J. Krailsheimer. New York: Penguin Books, 1982.

Peters, Jason. "Abstraction and Intimacy in Flannery O'Connor's *The Violent Bear It Away*." In *Dark Faith: New Essays on Flannery O'Connor's* The Violent Bear It Away, edited by Susan Srigley, 87–103. Notre Dame, IN: University of Notre Dame Press, 2012.

Phillips, Henry. "Pascal's Reading and the Inheritance of Montaigne and Descartes." In *Cambridge Companion to Pascal*, edited by Nicholas Hammond, 20–39. Cambridge: Cambridge University Press, 2003.

Pieper, Josef. *The Concept of Sin*. Translated by Edward T. Oakes, SJ. South Bend, IN: St. Augustine's Press, 2001.

———. *Tradition: Concept and Claim*. Translated by E. Christian Kopff. Wilmington, DE: ISI Books, 2008.

Piggford, George. "Flannery O'Connor, Friedrich von Hügel, and 'This Modernist Business.'" In *A Political Companion to Flannery O'Connor*, edited by Henry T. Edmondson, 101–24. Lexington: University of Kentucky Press, 2017.

Poulet, Georges. *Studies in Human Time*. Translated by Elliott Coleman. Baltimore, MD: The Johns Hopkins Press, 1956.

Ratzinger, Joseph. *Jesus of Nazareth: From the Baptism in the Jordan to the Transfiguration*. Translated by Adrian J. Walker. New York: Doubleday, 2007.

———. *Jesus of Nazareth: Holy Week: From the Entrance into Jerusalem to the Resurrection*. Translated by Philip J. Whitmore. San Francisco: Ignatius Press, 2011.

Saint Anselm. *Proslogion*. Translated by M. J. Charlesworth. Notre Dame, IN: University of Notre Dame Press, 1979.

Shaddix, M. K. *The Church Without the Church: Desert Orthodoxy in Flannery O'Connor's "Dear Old Dirty Southland"*. Macon, GA: Mercer University Press, 2015.

Srigley, Susan. "Asceticism and Abundance: The Communion of Saints in *The Violent Bear It Away*." In *Dark Faith: New Essays on Flannery O'Connor's* The Violent Bear It Away, edited by Susan Srigley, 185–212. Notre Dame, IN: University of Notre Dame Press, 2012.

———. *Flannery O'Connor's Sacramental Art*. Notre Dame, IN: University of Notre Dame Press, 2004.

Storey, Benjamin and Jenna Silber Storey. *Why We Are Restless: On the Modern Quest for Contentment*. Princeton, NJ and Oxford: Princeton University Press, 2021.

Ulanov, Barry. *Jung and the Outside World*. Asheville, NC: Chiron Press, 1992.

Von Balthasar, Hans Urs. Introduction to *The Scandal of the Incarnation: Irenaeus "Against the Heretics"* by Irenaeus. Edited by Hans Urs von Balthasar. Translated by John Saward. San Francisco: Ignatius Press, 1981.

Ward, Heather. *The Gift of Self*. London: Darton, Longman and Todd, 1990.

Wehner, David Z. "Pulverizing the Idols: Flannery O'Connor's Battle with Sigmund Freud and Carl Jung." *The Mississippi Quarterly* 65, no. 2 (Spring 2012): 299–320.

White, Victor, OP. *God and the Unconscious*. Cleveland, OH and New York: Meridian Books, The World Publishing Company, 1961.

Wood, Ralph C. *Flannery O'Connor and the Christ-Haunted South*. Grand Rapids, MI: Eerdmans, 2004.

Index

abortion, 62–63, 167–68
"A Good Man is Hard to Find": "good blood" in, 61; Grandmother's act of touching The Misfit depicts invisible action of grace, 92–94, 124–25, 132, 134, 148, 156, 172–73; The Misfit as prophet-freak, 94, 109, 162; The Misfit knows the incarnation necessitates a choice between good and evil, 19, 34, 92–95, 109, 127, 162–63; The Misfit's awareness of original sin and need for redemption, 19, 92–95, 101–2, 109, 162; The Misfit's diagnosis by Freudian psychiatrist, 19, 92; O'Connor's commentary on, 91–92, 94, 172–73; possibility of grace for The Misfit, 93–94, 109, 111; shows human condition at the end of the modern world, 162–63. *See also* guilt; incarnation; Jungian psychoanalysis; mystery; O'Connor, Flannery; original sin; prophetic vision
anagogical signification, 121–27, 149
Anselm, 127–28
Aquinas: on efficacious grace, 134n16; gloss on "the kingdom of heaven suffers violence," 133; influence on O'Connor, 5, 7; on prophecy, 124; on *ratio* and *intellectus*, 61n13; on reason's ability to remove obstacles to faith, 115n2; on senses of Scripture, 121–22
Aristotle and Aristotelian philosophy, 41, 95–97, 118, 119
asceticism, 133
Augustine, 5, 66, 133, 134n16, 135, 154, 169
autonomy, 62–63, 104, 159, 165–66, 168, 170, 172

Bacon, Francis, 54–55
Balthasar, Hans Urs von, 24–26, 164n14, 173n36, 174n40
baptism: spiritualization of, 59–60, 78; in *The Violent Bear It Away*, 76, 78, 82–88, 132
Bishop. *See The Violent Bear It Away*
blood: Enoch Emery's "wise blood," 28–29, 61; as "felt-knowledge," 27–28, 61; Hazel Motes resists and eventually accepts Christ's redeeming blood, 16, 27, 31, 34, 44, 139–40, 143; Hazel Motes's "wise blood," 16, 26–27, 30, 32–33, 61, 139, 150; Rayber and young Tarwater have "good blood" from old Tarwater, 61, 81, 82, 139, 150

charity: Christian conversion ends in, 20, 151–56; of Jesus, 20, 66, 154–56; modern culture reduces to compassion, 165–69; Rayber's irrational love for Bishop, 18–19, 75, 78–83, 85–86; and social bond, 170–72. *See also* heart
Christ. *See* Jesus Christ
Christian realism, 34–37, 38, 40. *See also unhistorical consciousness*
Civil War, 12
comedy, 19–20, 116–19
communion of saints, 16, 172
compassion, 165–69; dangers of governing by compassion, 169–70
confession, 109–11
consciousness. *See* modern self-consciousness
conversion: contrasted with psychoanalysis, 143–45, 152; ends in Christian charity and humility, 20, 149, 151–56; O'Connor's advice to converts, 4, 115, 127, 135, 151; and O'Connor's critique of sentimentality, 167; as recovery of the historical embodied reality of the incarnation, 137; as self-hatred, self-annihilation, or self-abandonment, 20, 43, 139–43, 145, 148–49, 151–52; as shifting of the center of existence from the self to Christ, 20, 138, 146–50, 152, 156; takes place at the level of the personality, 120, 125–26, 150; as transcendence of the merely psychological, 20, 143–48, 152
custom, 17, 38–39, 42, 140

Dante, 19–20, 116–17
deism, 96
Descartes, René, 3, 50n1, 96
detached and disembodied modern mind: depicted in character of Hulga, 18, 45–49, 51, 53–55, 67; illustrated by abortion debates, 62–63; Montaigne's self-consciousness as, 18, 49–55, 141; Pascal's recovery of the heart as response to, 18, 50n1, 61–67, 99–101; stance of objective observer-passive subject, 18, 49–60, 75, 76, 83, 141, 166
displacement, 19, 32, 94–105, 109, 158, 162
dogma, 17, 35–37, 124
dogmatism, 38
dreams, 51, 57, 107

Eliot, T. S., 8n10, 9, 37, 128–29, 171
Enoch Emery. *See Wise Blood*
Epictetus, 38
Eucharist: and bread of life in *The Violent Bear It Away*, 16, 61, 87–89, 166, 174; and divine hiddenness, 41–42, 174–75; as ground of mutual interdependence, 16, 173–75; reduced by modern psychology to a merely useful symbol, 107
euthanasia, 167
experiment: by Hulga, 46–48, 54, 166; in Jungian psychoanalysis, 69, 73, 143; as Montaigne's stance, 54–55; by Rayber, 76, 166

"felt-knowledge," 27, 28, 61
Foss, Jerome, 169–70

freaks, 19, 43, 94, 101, 109, 117–18, 162, 166. *See also* prophets

freedom: and modern autonomy, 62–63, 104, 159, 165–66, 168, 170, 172; as mystery in *The Violent Bear It Away*, 84, 86–89; as mystery in *Wise Blood*, 33–34; O'Connor's fiction shows characters' free choices of whether to accept or reject grace, 20, 120, 125–27, 150; Pascal on, 130–31, 134n16; self-consciousness seen as, 84, 165

Freud, Sigmund, 19, 56, 91–92, 129, 133. *See also* original sin

Gnosticism: contrasted with the Eucharist, 174; modern consciousness as, 5–7, 24–26, 61, 70; Rayber as "modern Manichean," 79; spiritualizes the incarnation, 6–7, 24–26

"Good Country People": Hulga's attempted experiment, 46–48, 54, 166; Hulga's intellectual pride and nihilism, 46, 47, 50n1, 101, 142, 153, 155–56; Hulga's lack of heart, 48–49, 61, 67; illustrates detached and disembodied modern mind, 18, 45–49, 51, 53–55, 67; O'Connor's commentary on, 47. *See also* detached and disembodied modern mind; experiment; heart

grace: effects change at the deepest level of the personality, 120, 125, 126; efficacious, 134n16; O'Connor on grace and nature, 15–16, 108, 120–21, 151, 172–73; O'Connor's fiction creates the experience of the possibility of, 4, 115–16, 125–26; O'Connor's fiction depicts invisible action of, 31, 92–94, 108–9, 118–27, 132–34, 150; O'Connor's fiction shows characters' free choices of whether to accept or reject, 20, 120, 125–27, 150; Pascal's view of grace and human freedom, 134n16; possibility of grace for Rayber, 83, 85–86, 94; possibility of grace for The Misfit, 93–94, 109, 111; role in conversion, 130–31, 137, 142, 146–52; shown in Grandmother's act of touching The Misfit, 92–94, 124–25, 132, 134, 148, 156, 172–73; and violence in O'Connor's stories, 132

Grandmother. *See* "A Good Man is Hard to Find"

Griffiths, Paul, 98, 142

Grou, Jean, 150

Guardini, Romano: on the church as bearer of authority, 37; on conversion, 130, 137, 141, 148; on the Eucharist, 173–74; on the heart, 62, 65–67; on humility, 155; on inadequacy of psychiatry to heal sin, 110; on modern culture's rejection of Christianity, 157–61; on Pascal's relevance for modernity, 9; on solitary modern consciousness, 104–5; on spiritualization of the incarnation, 40

guilt: as feature of modern consciousness, 1, 6, 23–24, 129–30; Hazel Motes's awareness of, 31, 139–40; The Misfit's awareness of, 19, 91–92, 94, 102; in Pascal's "true philosophy," 129–30; psychotherapy attempts to overcome, 91, 109–10, 129; young Tarwater's awareness of, 76, 86

Harari, Yuval Noah, 164–65
Hazel Motes. *See Wise Blood*
heart: formed by sacred tradition, 63; Hulga lacks, 48–49, 61, 67; openness to mystery, 63, 66, 99; Pascal recovers in response to detached modern consciousness, 18, 50n1, 61–67, 99–101; Pascal's "order of the heart," 154; as "wise blood" or "felt-knowledge" in O'Connor's stories, 18, 61, 65
hiddenness of God: in the Eucharist, 41–42, 174–75; in the incarnation, 41–44, 130, 140; Pascal on, 40–42, 96, 130, 140, 174
holiness, 145–46, 154
Hopkins, Gerard Manley, 151
Hügel, Friedrich von, 23n1, 98, 119, 147, 148
Hulga. *See* "Good Country People"
human dignity: modern culture rejects Christian ground for, 157–60, 163, 165; and trans-humanism, 164–65; in *The Violent Bear It Away*, 78–80, 87, 164, 168–69. *See also* incarnation
humanism, 167
humility, 20, 43, 140–42, 149, 151–56

incarnation: and divine hiddenness, 40–44, 130, 140; goal of Pascal's "true philosophy," 128; Hazel initially rejects but finally accepts historical reality of, 16, 17, 26–27, 31, 34, 43–44, 139–40, 143; Jung reduces to symbol, 7, 107; The Misfit knows it necessitates a choice between good and evil, 19, 34, 92–95, 109, 127, 162–63; and mystery of original sin, 129–30; and O'Connor's Catholic vision of the Protestant South, 15–16; O'Connor's fiction as "incarnational art," 61n13, 119–20, 174; as O'Connor's "standard of judgment," 17, 34–35, 43; Pascal identifies faith in a humiliated God as core of the Christian tradition, 43, 140–42, 155; rejected by modernity as ground for human dignity, 161, 166. *See also* spiritualization of the incarnation
integrity: of Hazel Motes, 17, 32–34, 133, 153; of the novelist, 36; role in O'Connor's comic fiction, 118, 133; of young Tarwater, 19
introspection, 55n8
intuitive knowledge, 64–65
Irenaeus, 25

Jansenism, 4n4, 10, 134n16
Jesus Christ: and anagogical vision, 120–22, 126; center of existence for old and young Tarwater, 15, 89; charity of, 66, 154; and Christian unity, 170; contrasted with the "god of the philosophers," 41; conversion as shifting of the center of existence from the self to Christ, 20, 138, 146–50,

152, 156; as essence of Christianity, 40; forgives sins, 111, 143; Hazel Motes's obsession with blood of, 16, 27, 31, 34, 44, 139–40, 143; Hazel Motes's process of conversion to, 139–40, 143, 150; and human suffering, 147; humility of, 20, 151–56; Pascal on futility of philosophy without knowledge of Christ, 96, 128; Pascal on the search for, 115, 138; and Protestant setting of O'Connor's stories, 14–15; Rayber's resistance to loving, 83; urgency of the choice about whether to follow, 130–31. *See also* Eucharist; incarnation; redemption; resurrection; *Wise Blood*

John the Baptist, 133, 135

Jung, Carl Gustav: on difference between the self-conscious elite and the masses, 164; on guilt, 91, 129; on intuitive knowledge, 65; on modern consciousness as "unhistorical, solitary, and guilty," 1, 6, 23–24; O'Connor's assessment of, 3, 58, 65, 91, 106–7, 145; reduces Christian mysteries to symbols, 59–60, 91, 106–7; on relation of psychoanalysis and religion, 56, 58–60, 106–7, 165; requires psychotherapist to suspend moral judgment, 110; on self-consciousness as means to preserve freedom, 165; on self-creation through self-consciousness as the goal of psychoanalysis, 18, 69–71, 73–74, 145, 165; on shifting of the center of consciousness, 73–74, 144; on social bond, 165; spiritualizes the incarnation, 6–7, 59, 159; on unhistorical consciousness as break with tradition, 6–7. *See also* Jungian psychoanalysis

Jungian psychoanalysis: in "A Good Man is Hard to Find," 19, 92; analysis of dreams, 51, 57, 107; attempts to overcome guilt, 91, 109–10, 129; contrasted with Christian conversion, 143–45, 152; contrasted with sacramental confession, 109–11; as outcome of early modern philosophy exemplified by Montaigne, 2–3; spiritualizes the incarnation, 6–7, 59, 144, 159; stance of objective observer-passive subject, 18, 55–60; in *The Violent Bear It Away*, 74–78, 81

Lake, Christina Bieber, 7, 26, 36–37, 77, 82–83, 85–86
Lewis, C. S., 171
Lewis, Helen Matthews, 7–8
love. *See* charity
Lynch, William, 35n11, 117–18, 122

Mahoney, Daniel, 167
Malebranche, Nicolas, 50n1
Manicheanism, 5–6, 79
Mauriac, François, 36n12
McCarthy, John, 67, 96, 103n12
McCarthy, Mary, 107
Misfit, The. *See* "A Good Man is Hard to Find"
Modernism, 23n1

modern self-consciousness: guilt as feature of, 1, 6, 23–24, 129–30; Jung's account of as "unhistorical, solitary, and guilty," 1, 6, 23–24; lacks sense of mystery, 19, 114–15; O'Connor's experience of, 1, 23–24; and Pascal's critique of Montaigne, 2–3, 8–9, 38–39, 102–5; as pride in need of conversion, 142, 155–56; sense of displacement, 19, 32, 94–105, 109, 158, 162. *See also* conversion; detached and disembodied modern mind; Montaigne, Michel de; solitary consciousness; unhistorical consciousness

Montaigne, Michel de: conflates "the good" with "value," 71–72; and detached and disembodied modern mind, 18, 49–55, 141; goal of self-containment and self-fulfillment, 18, 70–73, 102–5, 145; Jungian psychoanalysis as outcome of Montaigne's philosophy, 2–3; Pascal's critique of, 2–3, 8–9, 38–39, 102–5; reduces tradition to custom, 17, 38–39, 42, 140; skeptical of truth of Christianity, 38–39; spiritualization of the incarnation, 38, 53, 159; subjects inherited inclinations to judgment, 77n4. *See also* experiment; modern self-consciousness; reflection; solitary consciousness

Montgomery, Marion, 5–6, 12, 26n9, 61n13, 116

mutual interdependence: contrasted with modern solitary consciousness, 83, 89, 172; Eucharist as ground of, 16, 173–75; in O'Connor's stories, 12n18, 170–74; Protestant rejection of, 15–16

mystery: heart's openness to, 63, 66, 99; human freedom as, 33–34; Jung reduces Christian mysteries to symbols, 59–60, 106–7; The Misfit's grasp of, 92–94; modern consciousness has lost sense of, 19, 114–15; O'Connor's fiction recovers, 19, 105–9, 119, 123–27; original sin as, 92–93, 102–4, 129–30, 162; safeguarded by Catholic dogma, 17, 35–37, 124; in *The Violent Bear It Away*, 77, 80; in *Wise Blood*, 28. *See also* redemption

natural theology, 96
Nietzsche, Friedrich, 50n1, 154, 169
nihilism, 46–47, 50n1, 101, 169
nobility, 118, 133

O'Connor, Flannery
ON ART AND FICTION: acknowledges that she does not fully understand her own stories, 4, 124–25; on action and meaning in her stories, 4, 119, 137; on "Christian realism," 34–38, 40; commentary on "A Good Man is Hard to Find," 91–92, 94, 172–73; commentary on "Good Country

People," 47; commentary on *The Violent Bear It Away*, 15, 77, 81, 83, 85–87, 132; commentary on *Wise Blood*, 26, 28, 30, 32–34, 116; on the grotesque, 166; on "incarnational art," 61n13, 119–20, 174; on "thought-knowledge" and "felt-knowledge," 61; on violence in her stories, 132–33; on writing as self-abandonment, 148–49

ON CHRISTIANITY: advice to converts, 4, 115, 127, 135, 151; on being a Catholic in the modern world, 10–11, 161; on conversion, 20, 148–49, 151–52; on dogma as the guardian of mystery, 35–37, 124; on grace and nature, 15–16, 31, 94, 108, 120–21, 151, 172–73; on Jansenism, 4n4

CRITIQUE OF MODERNITY: on abortion, 168–69; familiarity with modern philosophy, 2–3, 7–8; on Jung and psychoanalysis, 3, 56, 58, 65, 91, 105–7, 143, 145; on "popular pity" and sentimentality, 166–67; shows limits of politics and dangers of governing by compassion, 169–70; on three types of modern man, 114–15

FICTION OF: addresses a skeptical and indifferent modern audience, 19–20, 114–17, 132; anagogical signification in, 121–27, 149; as comedy, 19, 116–19; creates the experience of the possibility of grace, 4, 115–16, 125–26; depicts invisible action of grace, 31, 92–94, 108–9, 118–27, 132–34, 150; embodies mystery, 107–9, 119, 123–27; freaks in, 19, 43, 94, 101, 109, 117–18, 162, 166; incarnation as "standard of judgment" in, 17, 34–35, 43; looks through the common and ordinary to the mystery of the incarnation, 11, 20, 117, 136, 162; mutual interdependence in, 12n18, 170–74; Pascal helps to experience meaning of, 2–4, 8–11; prophetic vision of, 121–27, 162; recovers mystery of original sin and redemption, 19, 105–9; recovers the reality of the incarnation from the distortions of spiritualization, 7, 10; sacramental worldview of, 14–16, 83, 87; shows characters' free choices of whether to accept or reject grace, 20, 120, 125–27, 150; transcends psychological explanations of human conduct, 20, 107–9, 120, 126–27; violence in, 131–35

PERSONAL LIFE AND EXPERIENCE: Catholic vision of the Protestant South, 11–16; experience of faith and doubt, 138, 143, 151; experience of modern consciousness, 1, 23–24; influenced by Aquinas and Thomism, 5, 7; physical suffering of, 147n19. *See also* "A Good Man is Hard to Find"; "Good Country People"; *The Violent Bear It Away*; *Wise Blood*

Oedipus Complex, 91

old Tarwater. *See The Violent Bear It Away*

original sin: and contrast between psychotherapy and sacramental confession, 109–11; and displacement of man in the modern world, 19, 32, 95–105, 162; as ground of Christian compassion, 166, 173; Hazel Motes's consciousness of, 30–31, 139–40, 143; The Misfit's consciousness of, 19, 92–95, 101–2, 109, 162; as mystery, 19, 92–93, 102–9, 129–30, 162; and need for constant conversion, 137; Onnie Jay Holy's "new jesus" as man without original sin, 29, 31; and Pascal's view of grace and freedom, 134n16; spiritualized by Jung and Freud, 91, 107; and subjective idea of value, 71

Pascal, Blaise: begins with experience rather than philosophy or doctrine, 38–39, 97, 128–29; breaks with pre-modernity, 10, 95–97, 127–28, 153; on Christian charity and humility, 149; on conversion as self-hatred and self-annihilation, 20, 43, 139–42, 145, 149, 163; critique of Malebranche, 50n1; critique of Montaigne, 2–3, 8–9, 38–39, 102–5; ethic of equality, 170; on the Eucharist, 173–75; on faith in a humiliated God as core of the Christian tradition, 43, 140–42, 155; on grace and human freedom, 134n16; helps to experience meaning of O'Connor's fiction, 2–4, 8–11; on hiddenness of God, 40–42, 96, 130, 140, 174; on human desire for eternity, 102–5; on the human will, 131n15; on inadequacy of modern science for study of man, 10, 19, 95, 97–99, 103, 128; on love of truth, 152; on man's displacement within nature, 95–105, 162; on the modern indifferent individual, 113–14; and modern view of personality, 158–59; physical suffering of, 147n19; on prophetic vision of Christianity, 42–43; recommended by O'Connor to converts, 4, 115, 127, 135; recovers historical reality of the incarnation from distortions of spiritualization, 7, 10, 17, 37–44; recovers the heart as response to detached and disembodied modern mind, 18, 50n1, 61–67, 99–101; "reflexive consciousness" of, 100; relevance for the modern Catholic, 8–11; scientific work, 9–10; on searching for God, 113–15, 138; on struggle and violence in the Christian life, 135, 147; on three "orders" of the human being, 154; on "true philosophy," 127–31, 153; on uniqueness of Christianity among religions, 40–44, 140; on urgency of the choice about whether to follow Christ, 20, 130–31; Wager, 20, 130–31, 151

Paul (apostle), 66, 154

personality: grace effects change at the deepest level of, 120, 125–26;

in modern culture, 158–59
Pieper, Joseph, 111, 129, 130n12, 170
pity, 47, 79, 166
pre-modernity: Catholic tendency to idealize, 10–11, 160–61; contrast between Dante's audience and O'Connor's modern readers, 115n2, 116–17; contrasted with modern culture, 158–61; contrasted with modern political thought, 169; experience of the mind, 49; in historical consciousness of the Protestant South, 12; Pascal breaks with, 10, 95–97, 127–28, 153; transition from medieval to modern philosophy, 8; understanding of man's place in nature, 95–96, 158
proofs for existence of God, 96, 127–28, 131
prophetic vision: and anagogical signification, 121–27; lost by modern culture's rejection of Christianity, 162; of The Misfit, 162; Pascal on, 42–43; in *Wise Blood*, 32–33, 44
prophets: Hazel Motes as, 32–33, 44, 150; in historical consciousness of the Protestant South, 13; The Misfit as, 94, 109, 162; old and young Tarwaters as, 74, 77, 82, 84, 87–88, 150; prophet-freaks, 43, 94, 109, 117–18
psychology: cannot completely account for mystery of human existence, 106–11; Christian conversion as transcendence of the merely psychological, 20, 143–48, 152; O'Connor's fiction transcends deterministic explanations of human conduct, 20, 107–9, 120, 126–27. *See also* Freud, Sigmund; Jung, Carl Gustav; Jungian psychoanalysis

Randall, John Herman, 8
Rayber. *See The Violent Bear It Away*
redemption: Gnosticism scandalized by, 25; as ground of Christian compassion, 166; Hazel Motes resists but finally accepts, 16, 27, 30, 31–34, 44, 139–40, 143; mystery of original sin points to need for, 93, 101–2, 103–4, 109, 129–30; and need for constant conversion, 137; O'Connor recovers mystery of, 19, 105–9; and O'Connor's critique of sentimentality, 167; parallel in process of psychoanalysis, 144; Pascal identifies faith in a humiliated God as core of the Christian tradition, 43, 140–42, 155; spiritualized as self-redemption through self-consciousness, 53, 60, 69–70, 78, 84, 145–46
reflection: contrasted with introspection, 55n8; means by which Montaigne achieves self-consciousness, 49–50, 52–53, 55n8, 62; Pascal does not begin from, 38–39
resurrection, 25, 59, 93, 106–7
revelation: distinct from intuitive knowledge, 65; and love of truth, 153; modern culture rejects authority of, 158–61; Montaigne rejects, 38–39; and

mystery of original sin, 129–30; Pascal defends eternity of sacred tradition, 39–40, 42–43

sacraments, 14–16. *See also* baptism; confession; Eucharist
scientific method, 3, 50n1, 54, 98
scriptural exegesis, 5–6, 121–22
self-consciousness. *See* modern self-consciousness
self-creation, 18, 46, 51–52, 69–70, 71, 73–74
self-hatred. *See* conversion; Pascal, Blaise
sentimentality, 166–67
social bond, 169–72
solitary consciousness: as break with tradition, 69, 73, 76, 84; in character of Rayber, 18–19, 74–87, 101; contrasted with mutual interdependence, 83, 89, 172; "inner transcendence" as spiritualization of the incarnation, 69, 101, 105, 149; Jung's aim of self-creation through self-consciousness, 18, 69–71, 73–74, 145, 165; Montaigne's goal of self-containment and self-fulfillment, 18, 70–73, 102–5, 145; self-creation through self-consciousness, 18, 46, 51–52, 69–71, 73–74; self-redemption through self-consciousness, 60, 69–70, 78, 84, 145–46
South, 11–16
spiritualization of the incarnation: and conversion as recovery of the incarnation, 137; "inner transcendence" as, 69, 101, 105, 149; by Montaigne, 38, 53, 159; as Onnie Jay Holy's "idea" in *Wise Blood*, 17, 27, 30, 139; Pascal and O'Connor both see their task as recovering the historical reality of the incarnation, 7, 10, 17, 37–44
Srigley, Susan, 114–15, 168–69, 172, 174
Storey, Benjamin and Jenna, 8–9, 103, 145n13
suffering, 146–47

Tarwaters. *See The Violent Bear It Away*
teleology, 97
Thomism. *See* Aquinas
tradition: and common culture, 170–71; dogma as the guardian of mystery, 35–37, 124; faith in a humiliated God as core of tradition for Pascal, 43, 140–42, 155; forms the heart, 63; Hazel Motes initially rejects, 17, 26–27, 34; in historical consciousness of the Protestant South, 14–15; modern consciousness as break with tradition, 6–7, 24, 36n12, 69, 73, 76, 84; Montaigne reduces to custom, 17, 38–39, 42, 140; Pascal defends eternity of sacred tradition, 39–40, 42–43; as "wise blood" in O'Connor's stories, 26–27. *See also* blood; unhistorical consciousness
tragedy, 117–18, 133
trans-humanism, 164–65

Jungian psychoanalysis, 6–7, 59, 144, 159; as modern Gnosticism, 6–7, 24–26; and modern unhistorical consciousness, 6–7, 24–26, 40; by Montaigne, 38, 53, 159; as Onnie Jay Holy's "idea" in *Wise Blood*, 17, 27, 30, 139; Pascal and O'Connor both see their task as recovering the historical reality of the incarnation, 7, 10, 17, 37–44

Ulanov, Barry, 10
unhistorical consciousness: as break with tradition, 6–7, 17, 24, 26–27, 31, 34, 36n12, 69; in character of Hazel Motes, 17, 26–27, 34; contrasted with O'Connor's "Christian realism," 34–38; in Jung's account of modern consciousness, 1, 6–7, 23–24; as modern Gnosticism, 6–7, 24–26; O'Connor's experience of, 23–24; and Pascal's recovery of historical reality of the incarnation, 37–44; and spiritualization of the incarnation, 6–7, 24–26, 40

violence, 131–35. *See also* grace
The Violent Bear It Away: baptism-drowning of Bishop, 76, 78, 82–88, 132; "good blood" inherited from old Tarwater, 61, 81–82, 139, 150; human freedom in, 84, 86–89; meaning of title, 133, 169; mystery in, 77, 80; O'Connor's commentary on, 15, 77, 81, 83, 85–86, 87, 132; old and young Tarwaters as prophets, 74, 77, 82, 84, 87–88, 150; old Tarwater's Christ-centered life, 15; possibility of grace for Rayber, 83, 85–86, 94; psychoanalysis in, 74–78, 81; Rayber as objective observer-passive subject, 75–76, 83, 166; Rayber illustrates modern solitary consciousness, 18–19, 74–87, 101; Rayber's attempt to reconstruct young Tarwater, 74–78; Rayber's intellectual pride, 142, 155–56; Rayber's irrational love for Bishop, 18–19, 75, 78–83, 85–86; Rayber's pity, 79, 166; Rayber's view of human dignity, 78–80, 87, 164, 168–69; reviewer's contemptuous description of young Tarwater, 13; shows O'Connor's sacramental worldview, 83, 87; Tarwaters' hunger for the bread of life, 16, 61, 87–89, 166, 174; young Tarwater's conversion to Christ, 139, 150. *See also* blood; charity; experiment; Gnosticism; grace; Jesus Christ; solitary consciousness

Ward, Heather, 146
White, Victor, 110, 144
Wise Blood: Enoch and Hazel's "wise blood," 16, 26–30, 32–33, 61, 139, 150; "The Eye," 45; Hazel initially rejects but finally accepts historical reality of the incarnation, 16–17, 26–27, 31, 34, 43–44, 139–40, 143; Hazel reveals unhistorical consciousness by rejecting the tradition, 17, 26–27, 34; Hazel's awareness of original sin, 30–31, 139–40, 143; Hazel's integrity, 17, 32–34, 133, 153; Hazel's intellectual pride, 142, 155–56; Hazel's process of conversion to Christ, 139–40, 143, 150; Hazel's prophetic vision, 32–33, 44, 150; Hazel's search for a "new jesus," 26–31, 44; mummy as man without

God, 17, 27–30; and O'Connor on herself a "hillbilly Thomist," 5; O'Connor's commentary on, 26, 28, 30, 32–34, 116; Onnie Jay Holy's "idea" as spiritualization of the incarnation, 17, 27–31, 139; violence in, 132. *See also* blood; guilt; incarnation; integrity; Jesus Christ; original sin; prophets; redemption; tradition; unhistorical consciousness

Wood, Ralph C., 13–14

young Tarwater. *See The Violent Bear It Away*